CHEYENNE

Produced
in Cooperation with the
CHEYENNE
Chamber of Commerce

Windsor Publications, Inc.
Northridge, California

CHEYENNE

Judith Adams

CITY
OF
BLUE
SKY

Frontispiece: A dramatic Cheyenne sunset silhouettes a lonely windmill on the plain.
Photo by Janet Hoffman Deaver

Windsor Publications, Inc.—History
Book Division
Managing Editor: Karen Story
Design Director: Alexander E. D'Anca

Staff for *Cheyenne: City of Blue Sky*
Senior Editor: Susan L. Wells
Production Editor, Corporate Biographies:
    Una FitzSimons
Editor, Corporate Biographies: Judith L. Hunter
Sales Representative, Corporate Biographies:
    Don Novis
Proofreader: Susan J. Muhler
Editorial Assistants: Didier Beauvoir,
    Thelma Fleischer, Kim Kievman,
    Rebecca Kropp, Mike Nugwynne, Kathy M.
    Peyser, Pat Pittman, Theresa J. Solis
Layout Artist, Corporate Biographies:
    John T. Wolff
Layout Artist, Editorial: Robaire Ream
Designer: Gary Hespenheide

Library of Congress Cataloging-in-Publication Data
    Adams, Judith, 1934-
    Cheyenne, city of blue sky / by Judith
        Adams. — 1st ed.
        p.   cm.
    Bibliography: p.124
    Includes index.
    ISBN 0-89781-229-8
    1. Cheyenne (Wyo.) — History.
    2. Cheyenne (Wyo.) — Description—Views.
    3. Cheyenne (Wyo.) — Industries.
    I. Title.
    F769.C5A3 1988
    978.7' 19—dc 19   88-22770
                                                  CIP

Windsor Publications, Inc.
Elliot Martin, Chairman of the Board
James L. Fish III, Chief Operating Officer

C O N T E N T S

To my family in appreciation for their
never-ending encouragement and patience.

Cheyenne has a country town feeling with a western flavor. Stetson hats and cowboy boots are everyday attire, "you bet" is a favorite expression, and the most popular vehicle is a pickup truck. Wyoming license plates, with the bronc-and-rider logo, emphasize the western spirit prevalent here.

Imbued from the beginning with the frontier values of self-sufficiency, integrity, fortitude, and independence, the people of

In 1906 J.E. Stimson photographed the rest house in Cheyenne City Park. Stimson documented every phase of life in the area from the turn of the century until the Depression. His work shows an excellence of photographic technique uncommon at the time. Courtesy, Wyoming State Archives, Museums and Historical Department

Cheyenne take an active interest in their community. Life is generally unhurried, and a friendly, straight-forward atmosphere prevails. The warmth and openness of Cheyennites, coupled with a genuine and active interest in local affairs, has created a modern city with a small-town feel.

Perhaps the best examples of Cheyenne's spirit are the homecoming parades down Capitol Avenue on Friday afternoons in October. People working along the parade route take a break to wave and shout encouragement to the local football team and cheerleaders.

The proud frontier heritage of Cheyenne is reflected in the small-town values and a "can do" attitude so prevalent in the city of today, a quintessentially old-western community in the new American West.

8

ACKNOWLEDGMENTS

I wish to extend my thanks to all those whose help make this history possible. While the limit of space makes it virtually impossible to mention everyone involved, I would especially like to thank Jim Birrell, photographic copies, and Paula West Chavoya, Supervisor of Photographic Collections, at the Wyoming State Museum and Historical Department; the staffs at Wyoming State Archives, Museums and Historical Department, Wyoming Travel Commission, and Wyoming Fish and Game; Sergeant Darin Allen West, Wing Historian, Warren Air Force Base; Tim White, Historic Governor's Mansion; Leclerque Jones, local Cheyenne historian; Mary Wegel, Superintendent of Schools office (secretary); and Carleen Williams, local Cheyenne artist, who painted the Crook House and the Corson House especially for this book.

Stockgrowers National Bank building was constructed in late 1905 on its present site at the corner of 17th Street and Capitol Avenue. It was built of native Iron Mountain sandstone, "of Roman architecture, modern in every particular." Known as First National Bank and Trust Company of Wyoming since 1964, the building has undergone several remodelings since its construction. Stockgrowers was founded in 1881. Courtesy, Wyoming State Archives, Museums and Historical Department

9

A Railroad Terminus
at Crow Creek Crossing

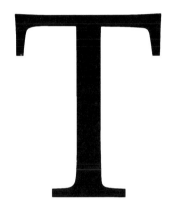

he site of the modern city of Cheyenne, Wyoming, was once an expanse of high plains, ending in the Rocky Mountains 30 miles to the west. This area was initially populated by Arapahoe, Cheyenne, and later Sioux Indians, nomads who wandered about the Great Plains hunting buffalo. The meat and hides of the buffalo provided food, shelter, and clothing—all the necessities of life. Once the Indians acquired horses, they used them to become better hunters and warriors. Stolen from other tribes or taken in battle, horses became the Indians' most valued possessions, imparting status as well as improving their means for survival. The Cheyenne called themselves the beautiful people. The Sioux gave them the name *Sha-hi-e-na*, which meant they spoke a language the Sioux could not understand.

A CHEYENNE LEGEND

According to a Cheyenne Indian legend, after a successful hunt an old squaw was too busy boiling bones and making grease to move with her people. As she worked on in the night by the light of a torch, Assiniboin Indians entered her lodge. They decided among themselves that they would enjoy a dinner before killing her. The Cheyenne woman fed them liberally of her boiled meat; then she put a great chunk of back fat on a stick over the fire and broiled it for them. When it was hot and dripping, she swung the stick in their faces, then ran from the lodge with her angry enemies in pursuit.

Running toward a cliff, the old squaw tossed the flaming stick over, turning sharply aside. Following the light, the Assiniboins fell over the precipice, and all were killed or

Facing page: This circa 1867 photograph depicts a construction outfit, typical of those working to put the railroad through at Crow Creek Crossing as well as at every other terminus along the route. Courtesy, Wyoming State Archives, Museums and Historical Department

General Grenville Mellen Dodge, chief engineer for the Union Pacific Railroad, chose the site for a railroad workers' camp at Crow Creek Crossing, and named it after the Cheyenne Indians who had once roamed the area. He laid out the streets for a four-square-mile townsite and had it approved by the new city council, after which land agents immediately started selling lots to businessmen and settlers. The "Magic City of the Plains" sprang up almost overnight. Courtesy, Wyoming State Archives, Museums and Historical Department

wounded. The squaw then went to the camp of her people, and they returned with her the next morning to find their enemies. They killed those who were still alive and took all of their guns. Thus, the legend concludes, the Cheyenne acquired firearms.

THE COMING OF THE RAILROAD

With the coming of the railroad, the years 1867, 1868, and 1869 were exciting ones for Wyoming. In the spring of 1867, General Grenville M. Dodge, then chief engineer for the Union Pacific Railroad, chose a site for a railroad workers' camp at Crow Creek Crossing and named it after the Cheyenne Indians who had roamed the area. Thus began the city of Cheyenne.

Previously, the 1803-1806 Lewis and Clark expedition had explored the area to find a route to the Pacific so that the United States could better take advantage of the western fur trade and establish commercial links with China and the Far East. In 1842 John Charles Fremont explored as far as the Wind River Mountains in western Wyoming. Congress passed a law in 1853 providing for a railroad route survey from the Mississippi River to the Pacific Ocean. This resulted in surveys of five different cross-country routes before the Union Pacific Railroad finally got the go-ahead to plow its way across southern Wyoming's plains and mountains. As incentive, Congress had made provision for land grants to the railroad, which it could disperse as it desired.

General Grenville M. Dodge, while on an Indian campaign with the army in 1865, had discovered Sherman Pass, a natural land bridge that extends from the open plains to the top of the mountain range, a distance of 30 miles. This pass was used for the railroad route through the mountains west of Cheyenne; later it would be used for the Lincoln Highway and eventually for Interstate 80, which crosses the northern United States from coast to coast.

At Crow Creek Crossing, a temporary city sprang up out of the plains almost overnight, earning it the name Magic City of the

Plains. Tents, shacks, and temporary buildings of all kinds appeared and were quickly occupied by gamblers, prostitutes, saloon keepers, merchants, and others attracted by the opportunity to separate the railroad employees from their weekly pay as quickly as possible.

Dusty or muddy streets, marked out by stakes, were deeply rutted by cart and wagon wheels and strewn with rubbish. A freight train arrived, loaded with frame houses,

This was a typical Union Pacific Railroad survey crew, a group of men who went ahead of the construction crews and determined the exact location for the tracks to be laid. Theirs was a risky job; two of these men lost their lives to an Indian raiding party, and their graves became a Cheyenne landmark. Courtesy, Wyoming State Archives, Museums and Historical Department

Cheyenne began as this tent town at Crow Creek Crossing in 1867. Tents, hastily erected ramshackle buldings, and even wagons provided temporary shelter for railroad workers, businessmen, settlers, and undesirables. Courtesy, Wyoming State Archives, Museums and Historical Department

lumber, palings, furniture, and old tents—all that was needed for a mushrooming city. The railroad guard said, "Gentlemen, here's Julesburg!" Julesburg, the previous terminus, had been broken down, stacked upon a freight car, and transported to the next terminus that would become Cheyenne. As soon as one town died, the next one, down the tracks, sprang to life.

General Dodge's plan for the four-square-mile townsite was approved by the brand-new, hastily assembled city council, and in mid-July James R. Whitehead, the company agent, began selling lots. The first lot sold for $150. Cheyenne's first settlers, six men and three women, arrived on July 9. When the tracks were still 20 miles east of Cheyenne, the population reached an estimated 3,000, and by the time the first little flare-stack engine steamed into Cheyenne on November 13, 1867, that number had swelled to 6,000. Most were adult males, but there were 400 women and 200 children as well. By July 25 the first house, a small frame structure, rose among the tents on 16th and Ferguson, which would later become Carey Avenue.

Cheyenne looked like a typical end-of-the-track railroad town, rough in appearance and in the behavior of its settlers. Tents and crude shacks were everywhere, and hard-working, hard-playing construction workers frequented the saloons at night. Upon his arrival in Cheyenne in August 1867, W.W. Corlette described the scene: "500 or 600 people were scattered around the prairie living mostly under wagons or in tents. I had my office with Whitehead in a tent, slept under a wagon myself for two or three months. Most everybody had come from Denver or other parts of Colorado; many had come for business purposes. Soon came the railroad builders and camp followers."

The city council held its meetings in one of the first row buildings, constructed by Judge William Kuykendall and James Whitehead in the 1600 block of Eddy Street, later renamed Pioneer Street and known as the Whitehead Block. The town's first known religious service was held in the same building by a Methodist minister in September, and committees of vigilantes also used this location for their meetings.

As the tracks extended west beyond the town, most of the gamblers, prostitutes, and other undesirables moved on to the next terminus, and by 1870 Cheyenne had settled into a more stable existence. The first school was in operation by February 1868, enrolling 114 students. The Union Pacific decided in 1868 to erect shops, a roundhouse, and a railroad hotel. Also in that year, the Denver

Judge W.L. Kuykendall was a former Confederate soldier from Missouri who arrived in the Cheyenne area before 1867 and was one of its first settlers. He and J.R. Whitehead built some of the first permanent structures in town, a row of buildings later called the Whitehead Block. The judge was instrumental in setting up Cheyenne's early government. Courtesy, Wyoming State Archives, Museums and Historical Department

Pacific Railroad line from Denver connected with the Union Pacific at Cheyenne.

In 1886 the *Cheyenne Sun* stated that Cheyenne provided one million dollars in business to the Union Pacific yearly, and its citizens felt the city deserved a depot of which it could be proud. The article also said that passengers avoided the present wooden depot as if it were a cowshed. The baggage and express office, supervisor's office, and dispatcher's office were all in separate buildings, creating much inconvenience. The article concluded that a new depot would encourage settlement by cattlemen and other businessmen in Cheyenne and the surrounding area. That year a new $90,000 depot was built, in a style known as Richardson Romanesque after U.S. architect Henry Hobson Richardson, noted for his creative use of local building materials. The building material used in the Cheyenne depot was polychromatic sandstone from quarries 50 miles to the south near Fort Collins, Colorado. The area around the depot was landscaped profusely with flower beds and shrubs. The depot was the largest, grandest structure in the territory, and its tower is still a prominent Cheyenne landmark.

Bill Bragg, in *Wyoming Rugged But Right* told the following railroad anecdote:

In its path across the country, the highest point of the Union Pacific Railroad was on Sherman Hill, between Cheyenne and Laramie. Near this point, at 8,235 feet of elevation, company officials erected a monument to Oakes and Oliver Ames, two brothers who had had a lot to do with the building of the railroad. The monument was a granite pyramid, 60 feet square at the base and 60 feet high. The granite, cut in huge blocks, came from a deposit about a half mile from the site. The monument took 50 men almost two years to complete, at a cost of nearly $50,000.

The Union Pacific depot, built in 1886, was the most impressive structure in the territory. Built in Richardson Romanesque style, it became a landmark to passengers approaching from the east after crossing miles of barren and windy prairie. Courtesy, Wyoming State Archives, Museums and Historical Department

Above: Elizabeth Rosenberg's sketch, from a Stimson photograph of Capitol Avenue in 1906, showed the new capitol building from the standpoint of the Union Pacific depot. The Burlington-Northern Railroad depot is on the right. Courtesy, Elizabeth Rosenberg

Below: The Union Pacific's "Big Boy" locomotive, the largest and heaviest single-expansion locomotive ever built, served the Union Pacific on the run between Cheyenne and Laramie over the Sherman Mountains. Designed by Union Pacific research experts for work in the mountains, these engines did the work of two locomotives. In the 1940s diesel power replaced steam on all railroads, and now a steam engine is a rare sight. This engine made its last run in 1958, and was retired to Holliday Park for public display in 1962. Courtesy, Wyoming Travel Commission

stock. Working with the soldiers at the fort were Pawnee Indian scouts. The Pawnee were traditional enemies of the Sioux, who were giving new settlers the most trouble in this area.

In the Indian Treaty of 1865, the United States had gained title to Cheyenne and Arapahoe lands to be crossed by the Union Pacific. The treaty effectively removed these tribes from the area. Another treaty made at Fort Laramie in 1868 set aside a hunting preserve for the Sioux far to the north and made it illegal for any white man to enter. The Sioux conducted raids from their territory, and hostilities culminated in the Sioux War of 1876. Abrogation of the 1868 treaty by the United States and recurrent Indian uprisings followed.

Life at the fort was relatively peaceful during the winter months, but exciting and dangerous in the summer. A common saying was, "Spring is here and so are the Indians." When the grass was five inches high, Indian raiding parties could leave their reservations to plunder, for the good grass kept their ponies strong and fleet.

In winter the Indians went back to the reservations, the troops came in from the field, and an attitude of good will and hospitality prevailed between the fort and town, where soldiers in cold-weather gear—overcoats made from tanned buffalo skins, buffalo shoes, and buffalo moccasins—were a common sight.

When there was trouble in Cheyenne, the troops were ready to help, whether it was a problem with construction workers or cowboys becoming too rowdy, or a disaster such as the fire of July 3, 1874. The fire broke out

This was the view from the Union Pacific depot tower, looking north up Capitol Avenue toward the capitol building. Public transportation began in 1887 with horse-drawn cars; these were later replaced by trolleys, as seen here in 1895. Courtesy, Wyoming State Archives, Museums and Historical Department

Meanwhile, a justice of the peace from Laramie found out that the monument had been built on a section of public land rather than on railroad land. He went to the public land office and filed a homestead claim on the section where the monument stood. Then he wrote to the Union Pacific in Omaha saying, "I would be greatly obliged if you would take that pile of stone off my farm!" A railroad attorney was sent to negotiate with Murphy to buy his land. Murphy was advised that it could be considered conspiracy for a judge to take advantage of his neighbor, and he might even be impeached. Murphy finally settled for two city lots, giving up his "farm" on Sherman Hill.

THE ESTABLISHMENT OF FORT RUSSELL

After the railroad terminal site was selected by General Dodge, General C.C. Auger of the United States Army was instructed to set up a military post for the purpose of protecting surveyors and construction workers from Indian attack. Unfortunately, despite this precaution, an Indian raiding party killed two men, and their graves marked the town site of Cheyenne. Approximately three miles northwest of the site chosen for Cheyenne, Fort D.A. Russell was established and formally named in September of 1867. About halfway between the fort and the town, a supply depot was established, referred to as Camp Carlin in honor of Colonel Carling (from the beginning, there was confusion about the spelling of his name). Its official name was Cheyenne Depot.

The first duty of the troops at Fort Russell was the railroad patrol. Every survey party and construction crew worked under the protection of the troops. There were escort parties for travelers and emigrants, and patrols that were sent out after stolen live-

In the mid- or late 1870s, railroad construction workers sometimes fought Indians to further progress of the tracks across the country. Courtesy, Wyoming State Archives, Museums and Historical Department

in downtown Cheyenne and, fanned by a strong wind, spread to several blocks. While this was happening, a message came from Chugwater saying an Indian party was on its way to free an Indian prisoner from the jail. Twenty minutes after the call for help to Fort Russell, cavalry and infantry were on their way to Cheyenne. The fire was brought under control, a trapped man was rescued from the roof of a building, and guards were placed around the town.

Personnel from Fort Russell joined in the first Frontier Day celebration in 1897 and have contributed to the celebration every year since then. The fort's cavalry troops rode in the parades, showing off their splendor, a practice that continued until 1927, when the fort became an infantry post.

Due to its strategic location near the railroad, Fort Russell was declared a permanent post in 1883, and the fort was rebuilt in 1885. In 1930 the name was changed to Fort F.E. Warren, in honor of the U.S. senator from Wyoming who served 37 years in office and was instrumental in getting appropriations for construction and maintenance at Fort Russell.

The fort was expanded in 1940 in response to the beginnings of World War II, and in 1947 Fort Warren was transferred to the air force and became F.E. Warren Air Force Base. In 1958 it became a Strategic Air Command base. Then came the siting of ICBMs: first the Minuteman and soon the MX.

THE HOSPITAL

Even before the railroad tracks reached Cheyenne, a hospital was set up at Hill (now Capitol) and 15th in a tent bought for $125. This facility was used until early 1868 when the hospital was moved to the second story of a wooden building on the corner of Dodge (now Warren) and 23rd. Doctors Irwin and Graham built the hospital, with room to house 40 patients. In 1869 the whole building was taken over by the city council and the county commissioners for a city and county hospital. In 1882 the county erected a brick-and-wood hospital building one block east,

Above: Fort Russell was established at the same time as Cheyenne, in 1867, to protect workers and settlers. The fort, later Warren Air Force Base, and the town of Cheyenne have always enjoyed a relationship of mutual support and help in times of trouble. The Fort Russell cavalry, shown here, participated in Frontier Day celebrations after its inception in 1897. Courtesy, Wyoming State Archives, Museums and Historical Department

Facing page, top: Although this building was constructed in 1882, B. Hellman had started his clothing business in 1867. His was one of the first businesses to be established in Cheyenne, while it was still a tent city. In 1984 the building was sold to L.R. Bresnahen for his Washington Meat Market. Courtesy, Wyoming State Archives, Museums and Historical Department

Facing page, bottom: This photograph shows Cheyenne's business section, along 16th Street, in late 1867 or early 1868. Some businesses were still in tents; others were in more "substantial" wooden buildings. Cheyenne's business community was already thriving when this picture was taken. Courtesy, Wyoming State Archives, Museums and Historical Department

at 23rd Street between Evans and House, on the site of the present hospital. It was named St. John's Hospital of Laramie County.

In 1902 Sarah Jane McKenzie, a registered nurse, took over as director of nurses, general superintendent, and business manager. She converted the run-down hospital to a modern one, equal to any in the West. McKenzie served for 23 years. A school of nursing was maintained at the hospital from 1901 to 1935.

EARLY BUSINESSES

As soon as the first settlers arrived at the new railroad terminus, merchants immediately set out their wares—on boxes near Crow Creek, in tents, in ramshackle buildings, and, by the end of the year, in more substantial buildings along 16th and 17th streets. This business district boasted twenty-five wholesale and retail groceries, nine wholesale liquor dealers, eight retail druggists, six jewelers and diamond dealers, eight hotels, six livery stables, and a furniture store. Three banks, three blacksmith shops, seven

Top: An early grocery store, which advertised "full weight, lowest price," butted against the one next door; the whole block was actually one building divided into various businesses. Dirt streets and board walks are evident in this photograph, circa 1890. Courtesy, Wyoming State Archives, Museums and Historical Department

Bottom: Nimmo Market in 1911 was a typical turn-of-the-century market, with packaged smoked meats hanging along the wall at left, a large scale on the counter, meat cases along the right, and a hardwood floor. Courtesy, Wyoming State Archives, Museums and Historical Department

lawyers, and six doctors were also part of the business community.

Newspapers advertised Louisville coal for $5.25 per ton, ice by the pound or the carload, beds for 15 cents, regular meals for 10 cents and up, warm or cold baths for one dollar, and 10 bath tickets for five dollars. A Turkish bath parlor, a Chinese laundry, a ladies' oyster saloon, cigar factories, and a carriage and wagon factory also advertised their services. One unusual ad said, "Wanted: man or woman to sell ostrich plumes." Cheyenne Steam Laundry, established in 1884, claimed in another ad, "We pay for all flannels shrunk in laundrying, no matter how expensive."

Frank Meanea, maker of saddles prized throughout the country and internationally, set up shop on West 17th Street in 1868 at age 19. He had served his apprenticeship with Gallatin, a famous saddler in Denver.

Barney Ford, a runaway slave, came to Cheyenne from Denver in 1867 and established Ford House, a hotel and restaurant. In the prevailing boom town atmosphere, Ford grossed $1,000 to $1,500 a day. His building was destroyed in the fire of 1870, which demolished much of the main business district. Ford returned to Denver, bought the Inter Ocean Hotel, and, in 1875, built a similar Inter Ocean Hotel in Cheyenne. Furnished elegantly with Brussels carpets, velvet chairs, and a carved mahogany bar, it was Cheyenne's leading hotel for many years. It ran a hack line to the train depot to transport patrons and their luggage.

In 1878 Ida Hamilton took advantage of prosperous times in Cheyenne and built the biggest and most pretentious brothel ever to flourish in Wyoming. The walls were of the best brick, windowsills and lintels were of carved sandstone, and the interior was lavishly furnished. Two large floor-to-ceiling mirrors in the front hall gave the house its nickname, "The House of Mirrors." Hamilton opened her establishment with a party, inviting prominent men by engraved invitation and importing girls from Denver to provide company for her guests. One of the girls married and moved across the street to Maple Terrace. Although propriety prevented her

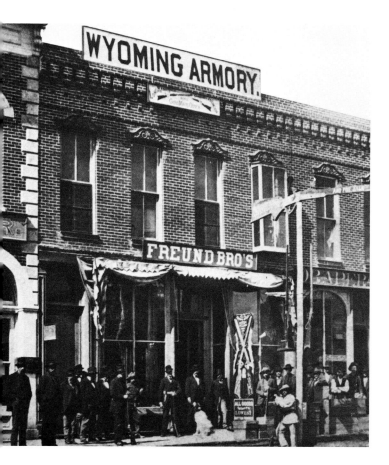

Above: These locked glass cases inside Frank Freund's armory in the mid-1880s displayed rifles and ammunition. The armory catered to a diversified population; the taxidermy on the wall attracted local sportsmen. Courtesy, Wyoming State Archives, Museums and Historical Department

Left: One of the important necessities of the day was supplied by Wyoming Armory, run by Frank W. Freund. By this time, around 1877, the businesses of Cheyenne were housed in very substantial structures, such as this typical brick building, butting against one another along the full length of the block. Courtesy, Wyoming State Archives, Museums and Historical Department

from visiting her friends, she did call across the street to get the news. Ida Hamilton retired, a wealthy woman, in the mid-1880s.

THE CHEYENNE-BLACK HILLS STAGE

The discovery in 1875 of gold in the Black Hills of Wyoming and Dakota led to the formation of the Cheyenne-Black Hills Stage. County commissioners contracted with George Homan, Jr., to establish a daily line of stages between Cheyenne and the Black Hills.

The Sioux Indians had possession of the area and were engaged in negotiations with Washington to open it up to prospectors. When the Sioux got to Cheyenne en route to Washington, they were treated royally and given gifts, including horses, saddles, bridles, lariats, and clothing.

The new stage provided daily service on the 300-mile route from Cheyenne to Dead-

wood; the trip took three days of traveling around the clock. Horses were changed and passengers could get meals at stations located every 15 miles. The coaches carried mail, passengers, and express deliveries. Gold was frequently sent from Deadwood to Cheyenne, usually in a special armored six-horse coach under guard by six armed messengers. This coach was often the target of road agents, who stole the horses and the gold. Some of the gold is said to be still buried along the route. On one occasion, a shipment of money was to be sent on the stage from Cheyenne to the Deadwood bank. The young wife of Tom Durbin hid the money in her baby's

clothing and delivered it safely. When she handed the money to her husband in Deadwood, he fainted. The previous day the stage had been held up and the driver killed by road agents who wanted that money. Exciting episodes such as this ended in February 1887 when the Chicago and Northwestern Railroad from Chadron, Nebraska, to Rapid City, South Dakota, was completed and there was no longer a need for traffic between Cheyenne and Deadwood.

A TRAVELER'S IMPRESSION

When German travel-writer Ernst von Hesse-Wartegg visited Cheyenne in 1876, he wrote:

We could not understand how a city of 4,000 could emerge in this place, a desert without trees, grass, or any other vegetation! . . . In all Cheyenne's environs, not a farm, not a house, not the faintest sign of culture. Yet here this important city thrives, the most important between the Missouri and the Great Salt Lake! . . .

These facts add up to a mystery. "The Magic City of the Plains." Cheyenne is magic indeed. But of the plains? Thirty miles west by train you cross the Rockies at 8,242 feet!

Cheyenne is another American miracle . . . ten years ago Judge Whitehead built the first house on the Cheyenne plateau . . . only ten years—and we arrive by Pullman Palace car and find the place a substantial, thriving city with friendly wide streets, splendid hotels, banks, jails, insurance companies, opera house and churches! Yes, churches . . . each faith has its own church in a city that, five years ago consisted of dugouts and moveable shacks. The shacks, portable on their little wooden wheels, made Cheyenne known as Hell on Wheels.

By the 1890s Cheyenne, the capital of Wyoming, boasted a population of 11,690, and its prominent industries included railroad shops, stockyards, saddlemakers, and wagon manufacturers.

Spirit, Mind, and Voice on the High Plains

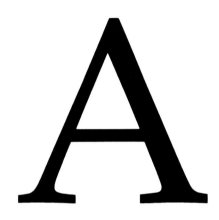

After the railroad moved on, taking with it the rowdy construction crews and attendant hangers-on and opportunists, the townspeople got down to the serious business of making Cheyenne a "decent place to live."

Ten years after its founding, Cheyenne boasted of seven established religious congregations. The Union Pacific Railroad issued building lots to organized church groups for the token payment of one dollar. Some congregations started building almost at once; others waited many years before they were able to erect permanent structures.

The area was looked upon as mission territory, and many church groups sent missionaries to establish a congregation in a new town and then move on to the next one. The congregations were left to carry on the best they could. Few churches had the luxury of permanent clergy and had to be content with traveling preachers or none at all.

A Methodist minister, the Reverend Baldwin of Burlington, Colorado Territory, preached a sermon in Cheyenne in September 1867, one month before the actual laying of railroad track into Cheyenne. Later the same month a Methodist society was organized by Dr. D.W. Scott. The Methodist Episcopal Church, later the First Methodist Church, is therefore considered the earliest permanent church organization in Cheyenne.

Two lots were obtained from the Union Pacific on the northeast corner of 18th and Central, and friends from the East donated $1,000 to build a church. Since there were only 19 members at first, the building wasn't started until 1870. That year, the minister and men of the church dug trenches for footings

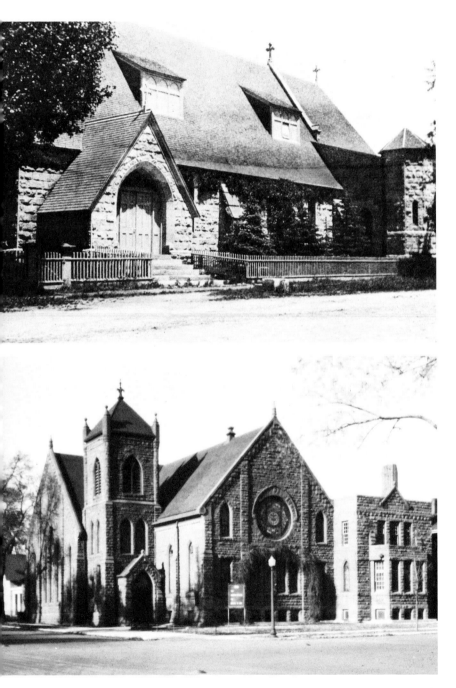

and hauled foundation stones from two miles west of the city. When lumber arrived from Chicago, a contractor erected the building on the foundation. In 1890 the frame church was replaced by the present stone building.

The Reverend W.F. Warren officiated at this church in 1876 when James B. "Wild Bill" Hickok was married to Agnes Lake Thatcher, a circus equestrienne. The pastor noted in the register of marriages: "Don't think they meant it."

In 1875 the African Methodist Church was formed by six blacks who had withdrawn from the First Methodist Church on Central. Lucy Phillips, who arrived in Cheyenne on the first passenger train in 1867 at the age of 62, donated a lot on the corner of 18th and Thomes. She lived to see the congregation well established before she died at 105 years of age. The little white-painted brick building served until it was demolished in 1982.

Faith Methodist Church, at 6th and Maxwell, had its beginnings as the South Side Sunday School, organized by a group of neighbors and held in a south side home in 1923. The church building was constructed in 1925, provided with a bell from the old Johnson School (which was being demolished at that time), and christened the Community Church. "Penny suppers" were served by the women of the congregation as fund-raisers during the Great Depression. The name and affiliation of the church changed several times: from United Brethren in 1930, to Evangelical United Brethren in 1946, to United Methodist in 1968, to and finally to Faith Methodist Church. Through-

Top: St. Mark's Episcopal Church, at 18th and Carey, was begun in 1886; the interior was finished in 1893. According to tradition, the church was patterned after Stoke Poges Church, Buckinghamshire, England. It was constructed of Castle Rock stone in the Gothic style. Its crowning features are the imported windows, including a Tiffany one. Courtesy, Wyoming State Archives, Museums and Historical Department

Bottom: In 1870 the newly appointed pastor of the First Methodist Church and the men of the church dug trenches for the footings and set the foundation stones, which they hauled from two miles west of town. A contractor erected a frame building, which was dedicated in September 1870. In 1890 that building was moved into the street in order to continue services, while a new stone structure, still standing today, was built on the same site. Courtesy, Wyoming State Archives, Museums and Historical Department

out the changes, it remained a neighborhood church; presently it is serving its third generation of worshipers.

During the summer of 1867, the first Episcopalian service in Cheyenne was conducted by a vacationing clergyman from Illinois. The Reverend Joseph W. Cook, the first resident rector, held services January 14, 1868. By the end of the month he had organized St. Mark's parish. It was named for St. Mark's Episcopal Church in Philadelphia, which donated $1,000 to the new church. Two lots were obtained from Union Pacific at 18th and Carey, and a wooden building was constructed; it was the first church built in Cheyenne from the ground up. When finished, St. Mark's boasted 26 comfortable pews, an organ, and a large bell. The bell still hangs in the tower of the present church. The Reverend Cook made the imitation stained-glass altar windows.

After a new church building was constructed in 1886-1887, the cross from the old building was suspended from the ceiling at the front of the new chancel. When the exterior and roof were complete, the church ran out of funds due to the cattle catastrophe. The interior was not completed and dedicated until May of 1893.

A women's organization of St. Mark's started a parish house, which became important during World War I when it held dances three nights a week for the entertainment of the soldiers at Fort Russell. Dances were 10 cents and the proceeds helped pay the church deficit.

St. Mark's has its own ghost story. During construction in 1886, two non-English-speaking Swedish immigrants were hired to build the tower and steeple, because they possessed the necessary Old World stone masonry skills. When the tower reached 40 feet in height, both masons disappeared. Later, during final construction, workers reported supernatural happenings. They convinced the rector, the Reverend Charles Bennett, to sanction the building of a "ghost room" in the tower just beneath the bell to appease the ghost, and, it was hoped, to end the strange tappings and muffled voices.

Academy of the Holy Child Jesus, opened in 1885 by St. John's Catholic Church, enrolled both day and resident students initially; later it became a boarding school, but this was discontinued when the building was demolished in 1952. Courtesy, Wyoming State Archives, Museums and Historical Department

Eighty years later, in 1966, St. Mark's rector, the Reverend Eugene Todd, visited an elderly man in a Denver nursing home who had been a colleague of one of the Swedish stone masons. He told how his friend's partner fell to his death during construction of the tower. Fearing deportation, the Swede hid his partner's corpse in the tower wall. The body remains unrecovered; therefore, the story is unsubstantiated.

Father William Kelly, having been appointed resident priest, arrived in Cheyenne in the late fall of 1867 and secured lots for a Catholic church on the northeast corner of 21st and O'Neil. A portable chapel from Omaha was set up in May 1868 and dedicated as St. John's Catholic Church. The priest's house and study were attached to the same building. Twenty persons were confirmed in the summer of 1869, and during

Construction of St. Mary's Cathedral at 21st and Capitol began in 1907, and the cornerstone was laid on July 7 of that year. Built of gray sandstone in the English Gothic style, the cathedral was enlarged and renovated for the Diamond Jubilee celebration marking the 75th anniversary of the Cheyenne diocese in February 1962. Courtesy, Wyoming State Archives, Museums and Historical Department

December of that year the first midnight Christmas Mass was performed at St. John's.

A growing congregation necessitated a larger building, and a new brick St. John's was built on the northeast corner of 19th and Carey and dedicated in May 1879. The old building was converted to a school and convent. When Wyoming became a diocese in 1887, the church was renamed St. Mary's. Cheyenne, as the see city, was the residence of the new bishop.

In 1907 a cathedral was built at 21st and Capitol; it was dedicated on January 31, 1909. By 1929 St. Mary's Cathedral had become too crowded and another site was needed for additional services. A Spanish mission-style church was built at 6th Street and Maxwell.

In 1938 a separate parish was created, and the church was named St. Joseph's Catholic Church.

Having requested duty in the "toughest town west of the Mississippi," a former Union officer, the Reverend J.D. Davis, arrived in Cheyenne on June 4, 1869. Eight days later a Congregational church of 13 members was formally organized in the schoolhouse. Reverend Davis is said to have remarked, "It needed more courage to plant the Gospel here than it did to hold up the old flag in battle."

Lots were obtained from Union Pacific on the northwest corner of 19th and Capitol. By mid-July $1,000 had been raised for a building, and the Reverend Davis went East and returned with lumber, paint, an organ, a small Sunday School library, and a wife. The new building was dedicated December 19, 1869. According to church minutes, a Union Sunday School picnic held in a grove 70 miles down the Denver railroad drew 515 Congregationalists, Methodists, and Presbyterians. They went to see the trees, because Cheyenne had "no gardens, no trees, and no weeds."

In 1880, after a four-week revival led by a Methodist preacher, 68 people joined the Congregational church. More space was needed, so in 1883 the church, enjoying financial prosperity along with the rest of Cheyenne, built a new brick sanctuary on the same site. The sanctuary, dedicated March 12, 1884, was one of the first buildings in Cheyenne to have electric lights. A furnace explosion in December 1933 ruined the interior of the church with flames and smoke. Services were held in the Masonic Temple across the street for a year while repairs were made. In 1954 five acres of land were bought for a modern sanctuary on East Pershing.

In 1885 the First Congregational Church organized a mission with nine members on the south side of town, at 12th and Evans. Known as the Railroad Chapel, the congregation was dissolved in 1906, although the building still served for several years as a Sunday School. After 1916 the building became part of the Union Pacific yards.

Zion Congregational Church, organized in 1923, originally held services in a building on 12th Street, until it had raised enough money to buy a lot and have a basement dug at 711 Maxwell. The remainder of the church was built by the members, working nights and Saturdays. In 1953 a new church building was erected at 600 East 7th Street, which adjoins the original property.

Although the first sermon in Cheyenne was apparently presented by a Baptist minister on August 4, 1867, the Baptists did not organize until 10 years later, on September 21, 1877, with 21 members. They met in various places: the YMCA, the Red Cross room, store buildings, private homes, and the courthouse. The members held an open-air baptismal service on May 5, 1880, at Sloan's Lake. Many of the townsfolk went out in carriages, and hotel buses ran a shuttle service enabling 500 people to witness the service.

On June 21, 1881, the Baptists were finally able to dedicate their brick building on 18th and Carey. This building was only used 13 years, however, for it was discovered to be unsafe. In the hurry to build, mortar laid in the cold winter months did not set prop-

The first Congregational Church, built in 1884 at 19th and Capitol, was one of the first buildings in Cheyenne to have electric lights. When a new church was built in 1958 on East Pershing and Forest Avenue, the handmade, imported leaded glass windows were moved from the old church. A special tower was built on the new site to display the bell taken from the old church. Courtesy, Wyoming State Archives, Museums and Historical Department

erly in the tower. The high part of the tower was later removed and a flat roof was placed on top.

An embossed metal-covered building was erected on the northwest corner of 19th and Warren. At the cornerstone ceremony on July 26, 1894, contractor H.Y. Mitchell sang in the choir and then put on his overalls to spread mortar. Unfortunately, paying for the organ, which had been shipped from California, was very difficult; also, the bell had to be returned for lack of funds. The present First Baptist Church was erected on East Pershing in 1955.

The Second Baptist Church, still serving its congregation at 1914 Thomes, was organized in 1884 by 10 black members of First Baptist. The present structure was built in 1949.

Missionary J.L. Gage organized the First Presbyterian Church with nine members and held the first service on July 10, 1869, in the schoolhouse. A small frame building, named Krebs Memorial Church in honor of a much-loved minister in New York, was dedicated July 17, 1870, on the northwest corner of 18th and Carey.

The First Baptist Church was erected in 1894 at 19th and Warren, in spite of the financial difficulties experienced by the congregation. This building served until 1955 when a new church was built on East Pershing. Courtesy, Wyoming State Archives, Museums and Historical Department

The ladies of the church actively raised money with oyster suppers, strawberry festivals, fairs, and musicals. By 1884 a brick church with a tall tower replaced the little frame building on the same site and was dedicated January 6. An imitation clock in the steeple had hands that pointed to 11:20, the time that Abraham Lincoln was shot. The interior was furnished with maroon Brussels carpet and Haverly opera chairs upholstered in red velvet. A quartet furnished the music for services, each member receiving one dollar a Sunday. The pipe organ was run by unreliable water pressure, and a boy was hired to pump for 50 cents a Sunday.

Demolished in 1921, the brick church was replaced with a limestone sanctuary in the perpendicular-Gothic style, with a tower and green roof. It was dedicated March 22, 1925. A mission-oriented church, it supported two native missionaries in Korea and China, starting in 1900, and also supported a church at Iron Mountain, 30 miles northwest of Cheyenne.

Pastor Henry W. Kuhns of Omaha secured lots for the First Scandinavian Evangelical Lutheran Church, known as the Swedish

Lutheran, from Union Pacific in November of 1867. The lots were to be held in trust for the church until it could organize.

In July 1884 Pastor F.M. Andreason, a Norwegian lay evangelist, came through the area and organized the first congregation of 31 people. The church functioned with the help of interim pastors, using the meeting facilities of other churches and organizations. Their Little White Church was finally built on the corner of 19th and House in 1888. As in most early frontier churches, the pastor was expected to serve more than one city, traveling to each on successive Sundays by way of the Union Pacific, which provided free passes to clergymen. In 1928 the church was fortunate to gain a student pastor, Conrad Floreen, who stayed until 1934 when he left to finish his education. In 1935 Emory Erlander became the church's first ordained, full-time pastor.

The name of the church was changed in 1927 to First English Lutheran because of the scarcity of Swedish residents in Cheyenne. In 1951 the name was again changed, to St. Paul's Lutheran Church. A new building was erected on the site and the Little White Church was moved to Place and Carbon streets, where it still serves the Free Methodist congregation.

German Lutheran church members originally met in the Swedish Lutheran building. In 1892 they were able to erect their own building, on the northwest corner of 20th and House, which served the congregation until 1952. That year they sold the building to the First South Baptist congregation and erected a new sanctuary at 1111 East 22nd Street, now known as Trinity Lutheran Church.

The first synagogue in Wyoming, Mt. Sinai, laid its cornerstone on October 23, 1915. A new synagogue, constructed in 1950 at Pioneer and 26th, is still in use. The old building became Frontier Elks Hall. It was demolished in 1979.

Cheyenne's Mormon Church, or the Church of Jesus Christ of Latter-day Saints, was first organized on March 16, 1926. Meetings were held at the Labor Journal Hall on 18th between Carey and Pioneer. In October

Originally, the hands on the imitation clock at the First Presbyterian Church pointed to the hour and minute of Abraham Lincoln's assassination. The church, built in 1894, was demolished and replaced in 1921 with a Gothic limestone structure on 22nd Street. Courtesy, Wyoming State Archives, Museums and Historical Department

of 1931, the church purchased property at 3011 Pioneer. A chapel at 30th and Thomes was constructed in 1940 and served the growing congregation as a meeting place for First, Second, and Third wards. It also functioned as the Cheyenne Stake Center until 1976, when a new Stake Center was completed at Western Hills and Education Drive.

Central School, on the north side of the 100 block of West 20th, was built according to an 11-year plan to replace the original frame schoolhouse. The first part was completed and occupied in 1871, and other sections were added in 1876 and 1881. Students who attended the school recall the innovative drinking "fountain" which consisted of two large rectangular tanks standing in the yard with iron cups chained to the front. The school was demolished in 1929. Courtesy, Wyoming State Archives, Museums and Historical Department

The Greek Orthodox faith was originally divided into two different groups in Cheyenne: the Sts. Constantine and Helen branch, following the Julian calendar, and the Holy Trinity branch, using the Gregorian calendar. In 1922 Gus Manelis, one of the original Greek Orthodox community leaders, organized a merger of the two groups. They retained the name Sts. Constantine and Helen and chose to use the Gregorian calendar, except when celebrating Easter. Father Elias Gerasimos served as the first priest. A lot was bought and a basement put in at 27th and

Thomes, with the remainder of the building completed and consecrated in 1936 under Father James Tavlarides. Today Manelis and Tom Ketcios, both in their nineties, are the only survivors of the original founders. According to Ketcios' daughter, Pauline Couris, this was the first Orthodox Church in Wyoming.

ESTABLISHMENT OF SCHOOLS

In October 1867 a letter to the editor appeared in the *Cheyenne Daily Leader*, followed by an article on the same topic, encouraging the development of a school to accommodate the growing number of children in the town. At the end of that month the city council appointed a committee to arrange for a schoolroom. There were 120 to 125 school-age children in Cheyenne at the time.

The first public school in Wyoming was erected in December 1867 on 19th and Carey and dedicated the next month. A former pupil recalled that "the first schoolhouse was a loosely built wooden shack of two rooms, seating perhaps 50 pupils each, through whose roof the first winter blizzard showered us with a fine mist of snow." Records show an enrollment of 114 pupils in February 1868.

In 1871 the original school building was replaced by a large brick structure, named Central School, on the block surrounded by Capitol, Central, 20th, and 21st streets. Soon after its completion, growth in the town necessitated more schools. Johnson School on the south side, Corlett School on the west side, and Converse School on the east side, were all built in the next decade.

The first school board election was held February 19, 1868. Chosen as officers were: S.M. Preshaw, director; Judge Kuykendall, treasurer; J.M. Pyper, clerk. School District

No. 1 was organized November 7, 1868, to cover an area of 270 square miles. Up until 1922 the district included six rural schools, in addition to the schools within the city.

Initially, superintendents were difficult to keep. School board meeting minutes mention M.A. Arnold as the first superintendent; according to differing records, he lasted either less than a month, or three months. He was followed by J.H. Hayford, who resigned after three days; Mr. Scriber; and finally, the

A class picture was traditionally taken at the close of the school year. In 1917, this elementary class from Johnson School took the annual event quite seriously. Courtesy, Wyoming State Archives, Museums and Historical Department

Reverend Joseph W. Cook, who held onto the position for about three years. Under the Reverend Cook stability seems to have been achieved, and subsequent superintendents have held their positions from 2 to 20 years. Those holding the office after Cook were: C.L. Morgan (1871-1872), N.E. Stark (1872-1885), J.O. Churchill (1885-1903), H.E. Conrad (1903-1905), S.S. Stockwell (1905-1912), Ira B. Fee (1912-1918), Andrew S. Jessup (1918-1938), Jessie L. Goins (1938-1955), Sam R. Clark (1955-1965), Chester Ingils (1965-1966), Loyd Crane (1966-1968), George Bailey (1968-1970), Joe Lutjeharms (1970-1976), Leo Beeden (acting superintendent, 1976-1977), and Dr. Byron Barry (1977-present).

There was also a high turnover rate among teachers in the first few years. Records show Mr. Stephen, Charles G. Wilson, W.G. Smith, Miss Marion G. Ellis, and the Reverend Charles L. Morgan, all of whom had completed teaching stints by the end of 1871 In school records, Superintendent Cook made the following notes:

May 17, 1869, Introduced George Smith as teacher in Cheyenne in place of Charles G. Wilson who has not given satisfaction.

May 24, 1869, Smith having gone on a spree, the school was closed.

May 28, 1869, Examined Miss Marion G. Ellis and gave her a certificate and permission to teach for two months.

Teachers were paid about $50 per month at that time, and schools were open four to five months a year.

The most serious problem in the first year was the difficulty of obtaining funds to run the school. A public meeting was called in February 1869 to address the problem. The *Daily Leader* of February 11, 1869, reported that "present indebtedness of the district for the expense of running the school was estimated at $4,000 and to raise the amount it was voted to levy a tax of five mills on the dollar . . . citizens are ready and willing to pay taxes to educate children." However, those same citizens balked at all other taxes and assessments.

A law making school compulsory for children was enacted by the Wyoming Legislature in 1869, but it was difficult to enforce. About 1872 Superintendent Stark wrote editorials appealing to parents, emphasizing punctuality and constancy as important attributes to be instilled in children. Stark's essays were not especially effective. He was a proponent of strict discipline; although he was once brought to court on assault and battery charges for whipping a pupil, he retained his position.

The first high school in Wyoming was established in 1875. In 1878 the first two graduates—both women—were Frankie Logan and Ella Hamma. The student body was predominantly female for the first 22 years.

In 1890 a pressed-brick and red-sandstone building was erected on Central at 22nd at a cost of $41,700. It served as Cheyenne High School until 1922, when a new school was built at Warren and 28th. The old building was converted to a junior high school, and in 1956 it became the administration building for Laramie County School District No. 1. It was demolished in 1964. Today, the administration occupies the building on Warren, and Cheyenne has two public high schools, Central High and East High.

In 1884 St. John's Catholic Church opened a school in the old church building and enrolled 100 pupils. It subsequently became a boarding school, Academy of the Holy Child Jesus. In 1952 the boarding school was discontinued and St. Mary's Grade School took its place. Later, high school grades were added, and in 1981 the high school was separated from St. Mary's and became Seton High.

Teachers' institutes met annually in Cheyenne beginning in 1874. N.E. Stark was one of the leaders in these institutes; the 1877 legislature required principals from all graded schools to attend. Many issues and

Cheyenne High School was built in 1890 on Central at 22nd Street. Girls used the main entrance facing Central, and boys entered from the back door. Basement playrooms for the boys and girls were separated by a room with four huge furnaces. The main stairway was of polished black walnut. In 1964 the 74-year-old landmark was demolished. Courtesy, Wyoming State Archives, Museums and Historical Department

problems were discussed, including the controversy surrounding the importance of vocational training versus traditional schooling, the argument for placing more emphasis on "our own vernacular—on history, literature, science and modern languages . . . instead of dead languages." Laramie journalist Bill Nye wrote:

There are very few households here as yet that can keep their own private poet . . . the crisp, dry air here is such that hunger is the chief style of yearning in Wyoming, and a good cook can get $125 per month where a bilious poet would be bothered like sin to get a job at $5 a week.

In 1886 Cheyenne, with two high school teachers, adopted a two-track high school program. Pupils could choose between a college preparatory course or a "business" course. Governor Thomas Moonlight, speaking at Cheyenne commencement in May 1887, urged the importance of obtaining a "practical" education.

Mothers' clubs gradually evolved in the schools, and a Parent-Teacher Association was established by concerned parents, mostly mothers, around 1914 and 1915. It provided a chance for mothers to relax, get away from the younger children and household chores, meet with the teachers, and talk about the welfare of their children. The schoolchildren dressed in their best and

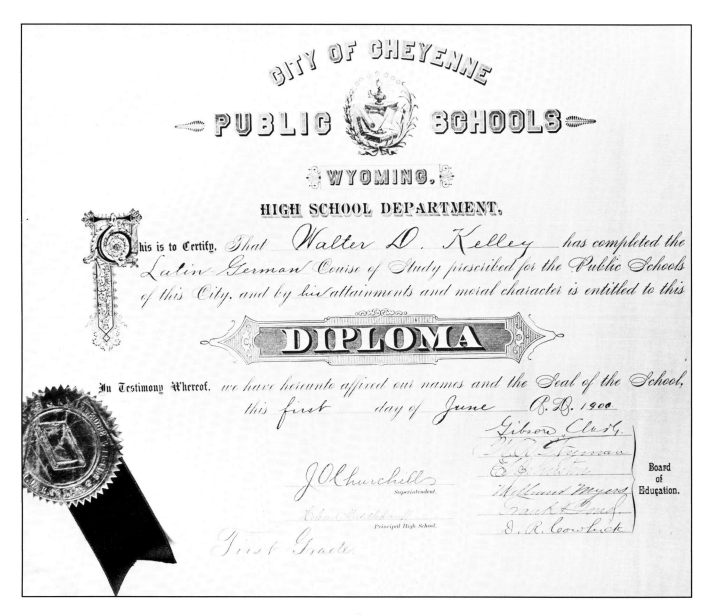

CITY OF CHEYENNE
~PUBLIC SCHOOLS~
WYOMING.
HIGH SCHOOL DEPARTMENT,
This is to Certify, That *Walter D. Kelley* has completed the *Latin German* Course of Study prescribed for the Public Schools of this City, and by his attainments and moral character is entitled to this

DIPLOMA

In Testimony Whereof, we have hereunto affixed our names and the Seal of the School, this *first* day of *June* A.D. *1900*.

J O Churchill
Superintendent.

Principal High School.

Board
of
Education.

This high school diploma from 1900 indicated the emphasis on foreign language study in Cheyenne at that time. Other sources indicate that the school curriculum included astronomy, philosophy, chemistry, algebra, geography, history, and music, in addition to the basic "reading, writing, and arithmetic." Courtesy, Wyoming State Archives, Museums and Historical Department

"spoke their piece" for the programs. There were art displays and tea and cookies as the mothers got to know each other.

Later they held evening meetings and invited the men. Everyone had so much fun that they arranged more meetings, appointed committees, and worked on projects. One of the main projects of the group was furnishing handkerchiefs for the children, as the boys were prone to use their sleeves and the girls their petticoats for runny noses. The women delivered 50 handkerchiefs per week to the school. All the members of the PTA were asked to donate rags, which the committee washed, boiled, pressed, and cut into squares. It was said they tore up all the old sheets and pillowcases in the town. One mother said, "We had no nurse in the school in those days, but we were beginning to learn about germs and we taught the children to cough and sneeze into their hankies."

THE CARNEGIE LIBRARY

Around the turn of the century, the citizens of Cheyenne became interested in building a public library to replace the library in the basement of the Central School. Robert Morris, Wyoming Supreme Court clerk and son of Wyoming suffragette Esther Hobart Morris, contacted philanthropist Andrew Carnegie, who contributed $50,000 for construction of the building after obtaining an agreement from Laramie County that it would provide a minimum of $3,000 per year for library maintenance.

In his dedication speech in 1902, Morris stated, "I know that I only voice the real sentiments of all the people of this community when I say that we accept this noble gift with feelings of deep gratitude. Let us be willing at all times to contribute generously towards its support, making it a power for good and the advancement of all that is best in this community."

When it was announced in April of 1971 that the Carnegie Library building would be demolished, Cheyenne architect Frederic Hutchison Porter commented, "That is and has been the most beautiful piece of architecture in Wyoming. It's a classic. It's a museum piece. I could just weep to think we're going to lose it." In this statement, he voiced the feelings of many of the citizens of Cheyenne. Mention of the Carnegie Library still evokes such sentiments today.

LARAMIE COUNTY COMMUNITY COLLEGE

"To help fill the need for technical training and post-secondary school education in

This photograph from Everett S. Hawes' collection depicts a Laramie County chemistry class in 1902. Courtesy, Wyoming State Archives, Museums and Historical Department

Above: Carnegie Library was built in 1901, on the southeast corner of Capitol and 22nd, at a cost of $55,000. It was demolished in 1971, and the Laramie County Library moved to its new building on Central Avenue and 28th Street. The Laramie County Library is the oldest surviving county library in the United States, legally incorporated in 1886. Courtesy, Wyoming State Archives, Museums and Historical Department

Left: In 1884 Alice Hebard became the first kindergarten teacher in Wyoming. She was well known as one of Cheyenne's pioneer educators, and well loved by her students. Hebard School was named after her. Born in 1859 in Clinton, Iowa, she died in 1928 in Laramie, Wyoming. Courtesy, Wyoming State Archives, Museums and Historical Department

Laramie County," Laramie County Community College was created on May 21, 1968, after voter approval. The new college, from its office at 609 W. 29th Street, offered an adult basic education course and graduated 19 students in June 1969. Various classes were added, and sessions were conducted in several locations, including church basements. During the summer of 1969, ground was broken for the college on 140 acres of land south of town donated by Arp and Hammond Hardware Company and Herbert Reed.

Enrollment tripled during the first 10 years, and in 1980 new construction was in progress to enlarge the facilities in order to

The first edition of The Cheyenne Leader *was published September 19, 1867; later it went through a series of name and ownership changes. Today this newspaper continues daily publication as it has in an unbroken line since its inception. Courtesy, Wyoming State Archives, Museums and Historical Department*

accommodate 3,000 full-time students. Today LCCC provides programs in continuing education, vocational and technical areas, and academic study. It awards two-year associate of arts and sciences degrees and applied-science degrees, transferable to a four-year college or university, and certificates of completion.

THE MEDIA

The *Cheyenne Daily Leader* began publication on September 19, 1867. The newspaper was begun by Nathan A. Baker and James E. Gates, who brought their equipment from Denver by horse and wagon.

March 3, 1876, saw the beginning of the *Cheyenne Daily Sun,* owned and edited by Colonel E.A. Slack. Slack was to become the most influential editor in the territory and later the state.

In 1884 the *Cheyenne Daily Tribune* began its long life under a series of owners that included Judge J.M. Carey, Wyoming's first United States senator. Its first editor, C.W. Ho-

bart, said of the paper that "in politics it will be Republican." Hobart was probably backed by Francis E. Warren and possibly Colorado Senator N.P. Hill of the *Denver Republican.* This paper in 1904 became the *Wyoming Tribune* under William C. Deming and James H. Walton.

In 1889 Cheyenne had three daily and three weekly newspapers; these continued well into Wyoming's statehood. Before that time, as many as 10 newspapers had appeared and quickly disappeared in Cheyenne.

In 1895 Colonel Slack bought the *Daily Leader* and began editing it, along with his *Sun. The Sun-Leader* was sold in 1920 to the *Wyoming State Tribune* under Deming, who came to be known as quite a crusader during his tenure. In 1908 Deming founded the *Stockman Farmer,* a monthly publication that remains an allied publication.

The *Wyoming State Tribune* changed ownership in 1937 to become the property of Tracy S. McCraken; in 1957 he turned it over to his son Robert, who still owns it today. The editorial page masthead of the *Tribune* carries, beneath its name, the names *Leader* and *Sun,* thus retaining an unbroken string of daily newspaper publication since 1867.

In May of 1925 the *Wyoming Eagle* was started by Joseph C. O'Mahoney (who would later become a well-known Wyoming senator), because he felt that Cheyenne needed a Democratic paper. Tracy McCraken bought the nearly defunct paper in 1926 and built it up from a struggling weekly to one of the

The Daily Leader *was established as Cheyenne's first newspaper on September 19, 1867. It was one of many publications merged over the years to form the present Cheyenne newspapers. The staff posing before the building certainly could not have guessed that its efforts would provide the basis for an uninterrupted chain of daily newspaper publishing to the present day. Courtesy, Wyoming State Archives, Museums and Historical Department*

leading dailies in the state. The *Eagle* was edited for many years by Bernard Horton.

In 1937 the *Eagle* and the *Tribune* merged under Tracy McCraken; his son Robert remains the publisher of both dailies, the *Eagle* morning edition and the *Tribune* afternoon edition, each with its own staff. In 1968 the combined *Tribune-Eagle Sunday Edition* was started, under a separate editor, and has continued to the present.

In 1935 Tracy McCraken sponsored a "Treagle" Train in support of the University of Wyoming and its athletic department. This became an annual event, with the train taking a load of Cheyenne businessmen to the university in Laramie (50 miles west of Cheyenne) for a football game and lunch. The state governor, the U.S. representative, and both U.S. senators were usually present, and each year some nationally known celebrity was also on the train. These notables included Drew Pearson, James Michener, Senator Ted Kennedy, Franklin D. Roosevelt, Jr., astronauts Gordon Cooper and Charles Conrad, Bill Moyer, and various motion picture and television stars. Except for a four-year hiatus during World War II, this unique event continued through 1979 when it was discontinued because of the group's expansion and the scarcity of railroad passenger cars.

Cheyenne radio station KYAN began broadcasting in October 1940 and was active for a few months. The Frontier Broadcasting Company began radio station KFBC in December 1940 and has continued to this day. KFBC was one of the first radio stations in Wyoming to become affiliated with a national radio network.

In 1945 KFBC organized the Wyoming Cowboy Network, featuring University of Wyoming sports and other special broadcasts, and became its key station. On these broadcasts Kurt Gowdy, nationally known sportscaster and a Wyoming native, began his radio career. By 1984 Cheyenne had three FM and four AM radio stations.

In March 1954 Frontier Broadcasting Company began Wyoming's first television station, KFBC-TV, on Channel 5. Cheyenne was the smallest community in the country

Colonel E.A. Slack began the Cheyenne Daily Sun *on March 3, 1876. According to historian T.A. Larson, Slack became the most influential editor in the territory, and later the state. Courtesy, Wyoming State Archives, Museums and Historical Department*

to have its own local TV station. It became KYCU in September 1972 when it was purchased by Wyneco Communications. Ownership changed again in December 1983 when Burke Broadcasting Company bought the station.

KYCU's attention to local coverage, community and regional affairs, and civic activities accounts for its long-time popularity. It was the first TV station in Wyoming to cover legislative events from the state capitol in Cheyenne, such as the governor's annual "state of the state" address.

Cheyenne came into being in July 1867. From the beginning early citizens of Cheyenne exhibited extreme commitment to the values of education, spiritual development, and community life. The first public school was operating within six months, and the public educational system presently goes up through the community college level. Seven religious congregations were already established within Cheyenne's first 10 years, and newspapers were operating within three months of the city's founding. The "decent place to live" was quickly on its way.

Magic City of the Plains at Work and Play

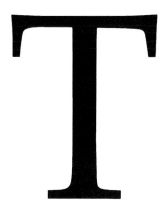

T he Union Pacific Railroad created Cheyenne; gold and cattle made it rich. When the railroad came to Cheyenne in 1867, it brought civilization and permanent settlers. These settlers had a different outlook from that of the homesteading farmers of previous frontiers to the east. Settlers arriving in Cheyenne were businessmen and investors, proficient at obtaining political power and wealth. Commercialism dominated the scene immediately.

Cheyenne was the railroad center for freight, passengers, cattle, and gold. In 1883 Cheyenne was so prosperous that 16th Street was referred to as "Wall Street." Cheyenne was the wealthiest city per capita in the world. With foreign aristocrats and eastern capitalists pouring money into the Wyoming cattle industry, fabulous homes were built in sections of town called "Baron's Row" and "Millionaire's Row."

The Black Hills gold strike of 1876 contributed to Cheyenne's prosperity, as merchants got rich outfitting prospective miners and relieving successful miners of their gold. Newspapers of the late 1870s and 1880s were filled with stories of gold shipments; gold nuggets and bars, gold dust, and jewelry made of gold decorated the windows of many Cheyenne merchants. Banks bought gold dust in lots of $2,000 to $10,000 daily.

Many of those drawn by the excitement of the gold rush later became famous; "Wild Bill" Hickok, Calamity Jane, and "Buffalo Bill" Cody were in and out of Cheyenne during those years. Outlaws such as Joel Collins and Sam Bass, Frank and Jesse James, and "Big Nose" George Parrot also became familiar names in the area, thanks to the frequent

Facing page: The Mandolin Club of Cheyenne was one of the many clubs in vogue around the turn of the century. Courtesy, Wyoming State Archives, Museums and Historical Department

Hiram B. Kelly, an early cattleman in the Cheyenne area, started a ranch on Chugwater Creek which he later sold to Swan Land and Cattle Company for half a million dollars. He married a half-breed Ogalalla Indian woman and built a large luxurious home in Cheyenne during the mid-1880s. The home was later sold to Mrs. Fred Boice and became a Cheyenne landmark. The barn became the Carriage House, a fashionable sports shop. The home was demolished in 1967 to make way for a state parking lot. Courtesy, Wyoming State Archives, Museums and Historical Department

Facing page, top: This large stone mansion was begun by A.H. Swan as a wedding present for his daughter, but when his cattle herds were wiped out in the 1887 blizzards, he sold it to David Dare, who finished it in legendary European style. Dare, connected with the Cheyenne National Bank, disappeared shortly before discrepancies were found in the bank's books. The bank failed and Dare stayed in Europe; he was never extradited. Of the mansion, only the carriage house at the rear remains, now occupied by government offices. Drawing by Elizabeth Rosenberg

Facing page, bottom: Cattle were rounded up in the Horsecreek area, northwest of Cheyenne, as seen in this circa 1880 photograph. During the open range days, cattle were allowed to roam at will to forage for food, and were rounded up when the time came to gather one's herd for sale. Ownership was determined by brand. In 1885, Alexander Swan, "The Cattle King of the West," ran 200,000 cattle. Courtesy, Wyoming State Archives, Museums and Historical Department

reports of gold shipments. Wyatt Earp was hired to ride shotgun on the Cheyenne-Black Hills Stage, and a special coach was designed to haul the treasure. It was lined with steel plates and had two portholes in the doors to permit defense of the treasure box, which was bolted to the floor.

THE CATTLE INDUSTRY

Even before the founding of Cheyenne, there were cattle on its ranges. The coming of the railroad brought more investors and enabled better shipment of cattle out of Cheyenne. John Iliff brought Texas longhorns to the area in February 1868 for a beef contract he had with military posts along the Union Pacific line. Hi Kelly, who had been in Wyoming for years, sold the first carload of live cattle to be shipped out of the state. Eastern capitalists and English, Irish, and Scottish speculators invested heavily in cattle, and the industry boomed, making Cheyenne the "cattle capital of the plains." Most Wyoming cattle barons lived in Cheyenne, and their stock ranged over an area half as large as the state.

A disastrous decline in the industry began in the winter of 1886-1887. A hot, dry summer followed by two winters of deep snows and blizzards, overgrazing, prairie fires, lax accounting, a price decline, cattle rustling, the inability of open-range cattle to find water—all contributed to the high losses experienced by cattlemen. Some reported losses of 80 percent, and many investors went bankrupt.

After the bust, the cattle industry was in transition. Better methods of cattle management, including watering and feeding programs, were instituted by stockmen. The number of cattle gradually increased, and the industry gained a firmer foundation.

In 1880 Alexander Swan introduced Hereford cattle to the area. He founded the famous Wyoming Hereford Ranch east of Cheyenne, which is still in operation. Swan was known across the country as the "Cattle King of the West."

As late as 1907 many residents of Cheyenne kept their own milk cows. The cows

A Cheyenne shepherd and his dog guarded the flock in 1912. The shepherd probably lived out on the range with his herd, in a wheeled "sheep wagon." Courtesy, Wyoming State Archives, Museums and Historical Department

were herded north of town for grazing in the morning and brought back home late in the afternoon. According to an early resident, staggered wooden poles were used for gates in the fence around Central School because of these cows. When residents planted new lawns, they had to protect them from the neighborhood cows, who liked to eat the tender young grass.

THE SHEEP INDUSTRY

The sheep industry was brought to Cheyenne by the Durbin brothers, who kept a herd near town in order to supply the meat market with fresh mutton. M.E. Post, of the Stebbins Post Bank, which received much of

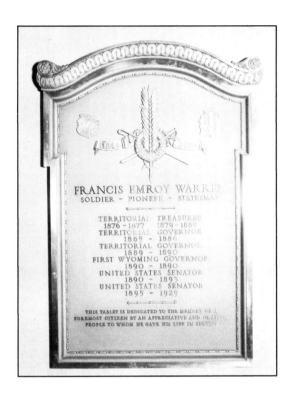

As a young man, Francis E. Warren came to Cheyenne in 1868 with 50 cents in his pocket. He acquired a large amount of land and founded Warren Mercantile Company. Later Warren became known as the senior statesman from Wyoming, serving twice as territorial governor, then as first governor of the state of Wyoming. He also served in the United States Senate for 30 years. Fort Russell was renamed in his honor. Warren died in 1929 at the age of 85. Courtesy, Wyoming State Archives, Museums and Historical Department

the gold from the Black Hills, was also in the business; he was called the "Sheep King of the Territory."

The 1880s witnessed steady growth in the sheep business, because sheep survived the winters better than cattle. Many cattlemen shifted their interests to sheep. The most famous sheep ranch in the area was started by Converse and Warren in the 1870s, and it later became the Warren Livestock Company, which is still in business today. The company developed a breed of sheep called Warhills, named after F.E. Warren and Dean John A. Hill of the University of Wyoming, who acted as advisor to the ranch.

Amasa R. Converse arrived in Cheyenne before the town was a week old. He set up a mercantile company and later became involved with F.E. Warren; their company was known as Warren Mercantile. That business has survived to the present, and is now known as Grier Furniture Company. Converse was active in the formation of Cheyenne's early government, and served as, among other things, treasurer of the territory of Wyoming. Converse County and Converse School in Cheyenne were named after him. Courtesy, Wyoming State Archives, Museums and Historical Department

"MILLIONAIRE'S ROW"

"Cheyenne is the headquarters of the 'cattle kings' of Wyoming," stated the *Omaha Herald* in 1875. That same year the *Cheyenne Leader* published a list of 19 Wyoming outfits with 1,000 or more cattle, as well as 51 smaller ranches.

Most of the "cattle barons" preferred to live in Cheyenne in their sumptuously furnished mansions rather than on ranches. Carey Avenue, 18th Street, and 17th Street became known as "Millionaire's Row" and "Baron's Row" for their display of large, expensive ($30,000 to $50,000) homes, many of them designed by George Rainsford, a local architect. The area enclosed by 17th Street, Warren Avenue, 22nd Street, and Morrie Avenue is known as the Rainsford district; many of its homes have been well-maintained up to the present.

Because of the railroad, architectural ornamentation was readily available, resulting in an eclectic mix of designs. Since the rail connected Cheyenne with the East Coast and therefore Europe, materials like Italian marble and cherrywood were available. Many of the mansions had stables; there are at least 100 barns and carriage houses still standing in Cheyenne. Inside the homes were paneled walls, cut-glass chandeliers, carved staircases, and several fireplaces, showing off the wealth of the owners.

The social life of the time was as extravagant as money could make it. Fruits and seafood shipped from the coasts were served at the best tables, and men as well as ladies dressed in the latest Eastern fashions. Cheyenne society was influenced by the city's status as territorial capital and later state capital; the legislature met there every two years, and the governor made his residence in Cheyenne. Also, Fort Russell was in close proximity. Military bands played for many private as well as public functions.

ENTERTAINMENT IN CHEYENNE

There were many variety shows in Cheyenne, especially during the "Hell on Wheels" days, and a decade later during the Black Hills gold rush. The shows presented

burlesque, with plenty of "lady performers." The typical variety theater provided entertainment, drinks, and gambling, all in one large room. A gallery where barmaids served select customers was over the bar.

The Union Pacific brought many of the best theatrical troupes of the day to Cheyenne, where they presented stage plays and operas. In 1882 Francis E. Warren built an opera house, its elegance rivaling that of the finest eastern theaters, at 17th and Capitol. It became the center of Cheyenne's theatrical life for the next 20 years. The opening-night performance by the Comly-Barton Opera Company attracted crowds from Laramie, Fort Collins, and Denver.

Roller skating and bicycling became popular pastimes in Cheyenne. A bicycle club was organized in 1882, and the *Leader* commented, "The untamed velocipede continues to travel about town, with one man on its back, and a dozen holding him there." Gambling was a favorite activity among men, whether it was formal as in games of poker, keno, faro, roulette, and dice, or informal, betting on boxing matches, foot races, and horse races. The *Cheyenne Sun* and *Wyoming Tribune* joined with the *Laramie Sentinel* in 1885 in a

Below: The Cheyenne Opera House was built on the corner of Capitol and 17th Street by Francis E. Warren in 1882, and became the setting for performances by traveling theatrical troupes as well as local groups for the next two decades. The theater boasted a seating capacity of 1,000; tickets were priced at 25 cents, 50 cents, one dollar, and $1.50 for the best seats in the house. Courtesy, Wyoming State Archives, Museums and Historical Department

Above: The Capitol Avenue Theater in 1905 typifies the opulence of the period. Intricately detailed wall and ceiling trim and plushy box seats were common in theaters of the day. Courtesy, Wyoming State Archives, Museums and Historical Department

The Cheyenne bicycle club shows off several styles of locomotion in this mid-1880s photograph, looking south on Carey Avenue from the corner of 17th Street. Courtesy, Wyoming State Archives, Museums and Historical Department

crusade to curb gambling excesses, but they made little progress. An abortive attempt to prohibit gambling was a major issue in the 1888 legislature. In 1901 the legislature finally prohibited gambling, but the law was not enforced and only served to force the gaming into back rooms.

Clubs of all kinds—business, professional, and social—came into vogue in Cheyenne. A Masonic Lodge was organized in 1868. Odd Fellows, Knights of Pythias, AOUW Lodge, Grand Army of the Republic, Sons of Union Veterans, Irish Benevolent Society, Pioneer Association, and Turn Verein Society (for those of German heritage) were all in operation by 1900. The Elks and Eagles lodges organized shortly thereafter.

A small number of women's clubs, five in 1890, gave women a chance to discuss poets like Browning and Bryant, play card games such as whist, attend high teas, and organize dinners and dances. Mixed clubs such as Twenty-one, the Pedro Club, and the Social Swim Club were also popular. Library, musical, and dramatic societies provided a cultural life unknown in other parts of the West. After the turn of the century, golf and basketball became popular for both men and women.

The New York-to-Paris automobile race passed through Wyoming in 1908. By 1913 automobiles were numerous enough that the legislature required their "registration and identification." This new mode of transportation made possible picnics and camping in the mountains 50 miles west of Cheyenne.

THE CHEYENNE CLUB

Cattlemen organized their own club in 1880 and built their famous and sumptuous clubhouse the following year. Briefly called the Cactus Club, it later became the Cheyenne Club. The club was originally limited to 50 members, who paid an initiation fee of $50 and yearly dues of $30. Military personnel paid no initiation fee but did pay dues. The clubhouse had a kitchen and dining room

Bottom: The New York-to-Paris automobile race passed through Wyoming in 1908. By 1913 autos were numerous enough that the legislature required "registration and identification" of them. This new mode of transportation opened the way for picnics and camping in the mountains 50 miles west of Cheyenne. Courtesy, Wyoming State Archives, Museums and Historical Department

Top: Dr. W. W. Crook posed circa 1900 in his Oldsmobile, reputed to have been the first automobile in Cheyenne. Dr. Crook was the first permanent physician in Cheyenne. Courtesy, Wyoming State Archives, Museums and Historical Department

The cattle barons' famous Cheyenne Club was reputed to be the grandest club between Chicago and San Francisco in the 1880s. Women weren't allowed inside, except to attend gala parties with Cheyenne's social elite. The building that housed the club boasted grand staircases and wine vaults, and delicacies were served from the East Coast, California, and abroad. The building is shown here in the 1920s after it became the home of the Cheyenne Chamber of Commerce. Courtesy, Wyoming State Archives, Museums and Historical Department

presided over by the finest chefs, a bar, a billiard room, meeting rooms, a smoking room, and upstairs guest rooms. Grounds for expulsion from the club included "offensive drunkenness," profanity or obscenity, a blow struck in a quarrel, cheating, a criminal act, or other behavior unbecoming to a gentleman.

The cattlemen could not maintain the club after their losses of 1886-1887, so the building was taken over by the Club of Cheyenne. The Cheyenne Industrial Club, which became the Cheyenne Chamber of Commerce, occupied it from 1907 until 1936 when the building was demolished.

CHEYENNE LITTLE THEATRE

In early 1930 representatives of 12 local service clubs met and formed the Cheyenne Little Theatre Players, electing Mrs. J.C. O'Mahoney president. A number of months before, the idea had taken shape at a card party attended by six theater lovers, including actors William De Vere and Barrie O'Daniels, and several members of the Cheyenne Women's Club. On May 7, 1930, the players presented their first production, and since then, excepting a three-year hiatus during World War II, the Little Theatre has provided Cheyenne with three to four quality theater productions every season.

The Cheyenne Little Theatre Players built their 290-seat playhouse on Windmill Road and Pershing in 1968. A summertime melodrama was added to their annual repertoire in 1957, and an annual children's play was added in 1970. In 1971 they purchased the historic Atlas Theater in downtown Cheyenne and have restored it over the years to its original turn-of-the-century style. The Atlas is now the home of the melodrama, with performances four nights per week during the summer months.

FRONTIER DAYS

The biggest event in Cheyenne is the annual Frontier Days Celebration, known the world over as the "Daddy of 'Em All." Beginning in 1897 as a one-day rodeo, it expanded the following year to two days. It continued to grow

Originally built in 1887, the Atlas Theater presented high-class vaudeville attractions. When silent movies replaced live performances, the Atlas became a movie theater. In 1966 the Cheyenne Little Theatre Players bought the building and renovated it, and now it is the home of their summer melodramas and dinner theater performances. Photo by Jim Birrell

Above: Cheyenne's annual "Daddy of 'Em All" began as a one-day rodeo in 1897. Since then it has evolved into a ten-day celebration with daily rodeos, night shows featuring nationally-known celebrities, free outdoor pancake breakfasts, parades with floats, horse-drawn historic vehicles, can-can dancers, marching bands, and daily outlaw vs. vigilante "shootouts" in downtown Cheyenne. Courtesy, Wyoming Travel Commission

Below: Organized Frontier Days parades began in the 1920s, and have since become one of the most important aspects of the celebration. The participants have been enthusiastic, and the parades well-attended, from the beginning. Courtesy, Wyoming State Archives, Museums and Historical Department

and today has become a 10-day affair that is at the center of Cheyenne business and politics for most of the year.

The first Frontier Day rodeo featured a mock-battle between the Sioux and the U.S. Cavalry from Fort Russell. Afterwards there were pony races, bucking horse contests, a pony express demonstration, steer roping, and a mock-stagecoach holdup, with vigilantes subsequently lynching the outlaws. Spectators who could not find bleacher seats stood shoulder-to-shoulder around the track or pulled their carriages close for seating. The following year, the two-day show included Indian dancing, a dramatization of the first election in Wyoming, and a dog-and-hare coursing event. That year William F. "Buffalo Bill" Cody led the first parade, composed of Cody's "Wild West" performers, horseback riders, Indians in their ceremonial costumes, a fire engine, and a mounted cowboy brass band.

Frontier Days was to become the biggest rodeo and offer the largest purse on the circuit. By 1908 Frontier Park was established, with seating for 7,700, to accommodate the crowds of spectators, many of whom traveled from Colorado and Nebraska.

Indians in war dance costume are ready to perform their ceremonial dances for a grandstand full of spectators at the "Daddy of 'Em All" in Frontier Park. Indian dancing was, and still is, a daily event during the Frontier Days celebration. Courtesy, Wyoming State Archives, Museums and Historical Department

The present-day "Daddy of 'Em All" consists of daily rodeos featuring barrel racing, bronc riding, bull riding, steer wrestling, calf and steer roping, and wild horse racing. Night shows feature Indian dances, chuckwagon races, and a main event, which has included such stars as Johnny Cash, Barbara Mandrell, Mel Tillis, Tammy Wynette, the Oak Ridge Boys, the Daniels Band, and many other country-and-western performers.

In the 1920s parades became a regular part of the celebration. The one parade of the early days has evolved into four huge parades today, winding around downtown Cheyenne for an hour and a half four mornings during Frontier Week. They include floats depicting pioneer days, vintage carriages and cars, precision horseback riding clubs, bands from across the country, the Coors eight-horse matched team of Belgians, dignitaries acting as grand marshal, costumed Indians, Miss Frontier with her entourage, and more.

In 1931 Jean Mimmo was selected to reign over the celebration as the first Miss Frontier. The rodeo queen has since become an integral part of Frontier Days, participating in the activities of Frontier Week and acting as public relations officer throughout the year. The queen is selected one year prior to

Left: Barrel racing is a major event at the Frontier Days rodeo, giving cowgirls an opportunity to take full part in the traditional celebration. The fast-paced sport requires flawless horsemanship and split-second timing, with most contests being won and lost by fractions of seconds. Courtesy, Wyoming Travel Commission

Below: Seldom seen in the United States, chuckwagon racing is a highlight of the Frontier Days night shows. The old range chuckwagons are pulled at amazing speeds by four horses while "outriders" attempt to maintain the pace. Drivers negotiate their teams through a figure eight around two barrels and then around the half-mile track. When the wagons make their final pass in front of the grandstand, everybody is up and cheering. Courtesy, Wyoming Travel Commission

her reign and acts as lady in waiting to that year's Miss Frontier. The following year she is crowned queen at a coronation ball and her attendant is announced. The queen is traditionally a descendant of a pioneer family and is of necessity a capable horsewoman.

The backbone of this 10-day wonder is a force of approximately 2,500 volunteers, organized into 10 committees. "Committee chairman" is a prestigious title in Cheyenne society. The general chairman, responsible for the organization of the entire hierarchy, is the only paid member. Frontier Days is held the last full week of July. In mid-September, after a six-week rest, the Frontier Days committees begin planning the next year's festivities; shortly after the new year, promotion begins nationwide.

Volunteers come from all professions, businesses, and social circles; beginning as workers on a committee, they move upward through the ranks for years toward the coveted chairman posts. Fort Russell/Warren Air Force Base personnel have also been involved in this community project since it began.

Also during Frontier Week, the Boy Scouts and Kiwanis Club put on three free pancake breakfasts in a downtown parking lot. Lines form for blocks, and from 8,000 to 10,000 people are fed each morning. Every afternoon, in the downtown outdoor mall, the Cheyenne Gunslingers stage a gunfight, to the delight of local and visiting passersby. Cowboy hats and boots are sold in great numbers, and cowboy bands play every night in most bars. The population swells with tourists, and many businesses make more money in those 10 days than in all other days of the year combined. The Frontier Days celebration involves everyone in Cheyenne in one way or another.

This four-horse team pulled a float during one of the early Frontier Days parades. These parades have become one of the big attractions of the celebration, occurring four times during the 10 days. Courtesy, Wyoming State Archives, Museums and Historical Department

A Modern City in the Equality State

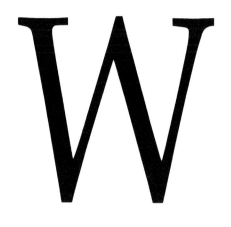

W hen the Union Pacific Railroad tracks reached Cheyenne on November 13, 1867, a provisional government was already set up. Originally part of the Dakota Territory, Laramie County was created in January 1867. When the city of Cheyenne was established by General Grenville Dodge on July 9, 1867, many of the first citizens were concerned about law and order. A meeting of interested citizens was held on August 7 to draft a city charter and organize a provisional government; the following evening, another meeting was held to adopt the charter. On August 9, citizens voted for city officials. A total of 303 votes was cast, electing H.M. Hook, mayor; R.E. Tapley, W.H. Harlow, S.M. Preshaw, J.D. Willis, and G.B. Thompson, councilmen; James R. Whitehead, city attorney; H.N. Meldrum, city treasurer; Thomas McLeland, city clerk; and E. Melanger, city marshal.

Another meeting was held on September 27 to begin organizing Laramie County. A full set of county officials was elected; Whitehead was selected as the representative to the Dakota legislature, and Cheyenne was selected as county seat. The Dakota Territorial Legislature granted a charter to Cheyenne in December 1867, and Luke Murrin was elected mayor. Residents were not eligible to vote unless they had lived in Cheyenne for three months prior to the election. Therefore only 1,002 votes were cast, although records show that there were around 7,000 people living in Cheyenne during 1868.

Wyoming Territory was established on July 25, 1868, by detaching most of the present-day state from the huge Dakota Territory to which it had belonged since 1864.

Facing page: Alert Hose Company was one of the early fire stations that served Cheyenne with volunteer firefighters. Others were Pioneer Hook and Ladder, Durant Steam Fire Company, and Clark Hose Company. Note the motto "We Strive to Save" in the stonework above the front window. Courtesy, Wyoming State Archives, Museums and Historical Department

J.R. Whitehead, considered by historians to be the first settler in Cheyenne, was chairman of the committee to draft a city charter in August 1867. He was elected the first city attorney; H.M. Hook was the first mayor. Courtesy, Wyoming State Archives, Museums and Historical Department

Wyoming's first territorial governor, John A. Campbell, designated Cheyenne as temporary capital. In 1901 it became the permanent state capital.

EARLY JUSTICE

Justice in Cheyenne in its early days was handled by vigilante committees. On one occasion three men were arrested by the U.S. marshal and charged with stealing $900. The prisoners were put under bond to appear before the U.S. commissioner, then set at liberty. The following morning they were found on Pioneer Avenue, tied together, with a sign that read: "$900 stole, $500 returned. Thieves. F. St. Clair, W. Grier, E.D. Brownville. City authorities please do not interfere until 10 o'clock p.m. Next case goes up a tree. Beware of Vigilance Committee."

Although the committee generated much interest and excitement, records show only two men were actually lynched. By early 1868, with establishment of city government, a police force, and courts, the vigilantes were no longer necessary. The marshal was appointed chief of police and allowed to select two policemen. Offenders were to be put in irons and guarded until a jail could be constructed. Later a log cabin on Thomes was converted to a jail for tramps and petty offenders. When the one-room structure became full, a semi-official mob took the occupants out one at a time, asked each where he wished to go, turned him in that direction, and helped him get started with the aid of a whip or six-gun kicking dirt around his heels.

Before a formal jail existed, according to Bill Bragg, two cowboys were arrested in Cheyenne and placed by a tough marshal named Luke Vorhees in a tent with the word "jail" painted on it. The prisoners awoke some hours later with massive hangovers, suffering from extreme thirst. They picked up the tent and moved it several miles to the bank of Crow Creek where they satisfied their thirst. When the marshal finally found his jail, the prisoners explained that, rather than break out of the jail, they just took it with them. The marshal let them off with a warning.

The records of the county clerk contain an agreement dated August 21, 1867, concerning the building of a jail in Cheyenne. Called "Plans and Specifications for Jail Building," it states that the jail should be 20 feet square by eight feet high, of "sawed lumber six inches thick of a uniform width, not less than ten inches wide," and should have "well nailed down floorboards." The jail building was built on October 3, 1867, for a total cost of $1,645.

Construction of a Laramie County Court-house and jail was authorized in 1872. The county then extended from Colorado to Montana, but there were few white settlers north of the North Platte River. The jail and court-house, located at the corner of 19th and Carey, were demolished around 1917 to make way for construction of the present Laramie County Courthouse.

When Wyoming became a territory in 1869, its own judiciary began to function. There were three judicial districts, each presided over by a federally appointed judge

Top: Along 18th Street between Capitol and Central Avenues in 1932 stood four homes and a fine boarding house; this was known as Cottage Row. One of the homes belonged to William Hale, governor of Wyoming Territory from 1882 to 1885. His house, the last of the group to remain standing, later became a popular teahouse called "The Gables." It was removed about 1941 to make way for the offices of Cheyenne Light, Fuel, and Power. Courtesy, Wyoming State Archives, Museums and Historical Department

Bottom: The Laramie County courthouse was built jointly by the City of Cheyenne and Laramie County in 1919 and was known as the City-County building. After city offices were moved to a new municipal building in 1979, this building was restored and renovated for use as the Laramie County courthouse and office building. It is one of the last examples of neo-classical architecture left in Cheyenne. Courtesy, Wyoming State Archives, Museums and Historical Department

Left: Joseph Maul Carey arrived in Cheyenne in 1869, having been appointed United States attorney for the new territory of Wyoming. In subsequent years he served as assistant justice of the supreme court, territorial delegate to Congress, United States senator from the new state of Wyoming, and Wyoming governor. He died in 1924 at the age of 79. Courtesy, Wyoming State Archives, Museums and Historical Department

Below: When Joseph Maul Carey built this house in 1885, it was the largest and most elaborate home on Ferguson Street, now Carey Avenue. It was three stories high and featured large porches, bay windows, a spacious and beautiful interior, massive fireplaces, crystal chandeliers, and frescoed ceilings done by an Italian artist imported by Carey. The parquet floors were partially covered by Oriental rugs and gold embossed paper covered some of the walls. The house served as the governor's mansion during Carey's term in office. A modern post office now occupies the site. Courtesy, Wyoming State Archives, Museums and Historical Department

who rode the circuit and heard cases. The three judges met in Cheyenne once a year to consider the appeals that had taken place in their trial courts and, as a disgruntled lawyer said, "to affirm each other's errors."

This judicial system continued until Wyoming became a state in 1890. The judges, appointed by the president, had a great deal of power and were not popular, probably because they were political imports.

During railroad construction, enforcement of the law was difficult until crews moved on to the next town. The gang of construction workers and assorted "hangers-on" earned the label "Hell on Wheels"; they were joined by gamblers, saloon keepers, and various gun-toters in flouting the laws of the town. Occasionally officers from Fort Russell helped to maintain order in town. At one point, General Dodge called for help from General J.E. Stevenson, commander at the fort. The general and his soldiers ran the entire population out of town to a point about a mile south of Cheyenne, had a parley with them, and permitted them to return only after they agreed to be more orderly.

Anxious to promote Wyoming's development, the first territorial legislature enacted a law in 1869 giving women the right to vote and hold office. First Chief Justice John H. Howe decreed that if women could vote and hold office, they could also sit on juries. His ruling became the subject of news dispatches around the world; King William of Prussia cabled congratulations to President Ulysses S. Grant, citing the "progress, enlightenment and civil liberty in America."

The first trial with female jury members was held in Laramie and created much dissension. Cartoonists depicted the women bouncing fretting babies while they heard the evidence. One caption read, "Baby, baby, don't get in a fury; your mama's gone to sit on the jury." Women did not sit on juries again until after the 1869 law was amended in 1949.

Also in 1869, Esther Hobart Morris, well-known proponent of the women's suffrage movement, was commissioned justice of the peace. Although she served only eight and a half months, she passed the test of holding

W.W. Slaughter, one of the pioneer organizers of Cheyenne city government, served as mayor in 1869. Courtesy, Wyoming State Archives, Museums and Historical Department

Top: This residential section of 18th Street in midtown Cheyenne looks much the same today as it did in this 1904 photo, with huge cottonwood trees shading Victorian-style homes. Courtesy, Wyoming State Archives, Museums and Historical Department

Bottom: Spruced up and ready for a note-worthy occasion, members of a family pose on the porch of their Victorian-style home in Cheyenne around 1920. Courtesy, Wyoming State Archives, Museums and Historical Department

public office. Her statue stands before the Wyoming State Capitol.

Esther Morris is historically given credit for passage of a women's suffrage bill in Wyoming, but the bill was actually authored by William H. Bright, who, some historians contend, was heavily influenced by his wife Julia. Various Cheyenne women worked for suffrage, among them Mrs. M.E. Post, who had come west in a covered wagon, married

the part-owner of Stebbins Post Bank, and lived in an elegantly furnished Victorian home on Carey Avenue. Post presented the suffrage petition to a constitutional convention in 1889.

Although women had been given the right to vote and hold office in the territory, an attempt was made to repeal the act at the constitutional convention held in September 1889, in preparation for statehood. Theresa Jenkins hitched up her horse and buggy and called on every woman in Cheyenne, urging them to assemble at the capitol, where the legislature was in session, and insist that their rights be retained. This they did, and women's suffrage was saved for Wyoming. By six that evening, Jenkins had returned home to give birth to a baby girl. When she was later granted the honor of delivering the Statehood Address, Jenkins rehearsed her speech on the open prairie, while her husband rode his buggy off to greater and greater distances, periodically shouting back to her, "Louder . . . louder."

The territorial legislature approved construction of a capitol building in 1886. Cornerstone ceremonies were held May 18, 1887, and the main part of the building was completed in March 1888. Wings on each end of the original structure were completed in April 1890, in time for statehood, which was conferred upon Wyoming by President Benjamin Harrison on July 10, 1890. Thus Wyoming became the 44th state, with Cheyenne its capital city. The gleaming new building on Capitol Avenue housed the state government. The first census reported

Wyoming's population at 62,555, including 1,850 Indians on reservations.

TOM HORN

Tom Horn, a former Pinkerton agent and stock detective, was credited with the murders of several men in Wyoming and Colorado who had been suspected of stealing cattle. His reputation was such that mothers warned their children, "One day Tom Horn will get you if you stay out after dark."

One victim, 13-year-old Willie Nickell, was shot and killed in 1901, apparently mistaken for his father. Later his father was shot several times and wounded. While under the influence of liquor, Tom Horn bragged about committing the crime. Deputy U.S. Marshal Joe LeFors had a secretary secretly make notes of the conversation between LeFors and Horn, and it was that "confession," Horn's reputation, and public opinion that convicted Horn in 1902.

Horn escaped but was recaptured after eight months. Before he was hanged, there was a great deal of excitement and conjecture among the citizens, as a number of cattlemen might have been implicated. Pressure was even brought to bear upon Governor

Top: The cornerstone for the Wyoming territorial capitol building was laid on May 18, 1887. At the same time, the name of Hill Street was changed to Capitol Avenue, and the cornerstone-laying ceremony culminated in a celebratory barbecue. The clock tower for the new Union Pacific depot was also going up at the south end of Capitol Avenue. In January 1888 the territorial legislature began meeting in the new capitol building. Courtesy, Wyoming State Archives, Museums and Historical Department

Bottom: This log house, moved into Cheyenne and reassembled, was originally the ranch home of George W. Baxter, who served as governor of Wyoming Territory for 45 days in 1886. He resigned over a dispute concerning his fenced land, which included some government land—government sections alternated with private sections along the railroad. He was later exonerated but was not restored to office. Courtesy, Wyoming State Archives, Museums and Historical Department

Above: After the formation of a paid fire department, the former Alert Hose Company building was occupied by Cheyenne Light, Fuel, and Power Company and an insurance company. The old firefighter's motto chiseled in stone above the window—We Strive to Save—continued to be appropriate. The building was demolished in 1960. Courtesy, Wyoming State Archives, Museums and Historical Department

Facing page, top: In May 1903 President Theodore Roosevelt arrived in Laramie by train and rode horseback with a group of men to Cheyenne—approximately a 50-mile trek—to attend a dinner at F.E. Warren's Terry Ranch south of Cheyenne. United States Senator F.E. Warren is shown third from the left; the group on the right is led by Roosevelt, and among that group is Joe LeFors, the United States marshal who heard Tom Horn's "confession." Courtesy, Wyoming State Archives, Museums and Historical Department

Facing page, bottom: Theodore Roosevelt and Wyoming Governor B. Brooks are shown in Cheyenne during Roosevelt's visit to Wyoming in 1910. During his presidency, Roosevelt worked for land reclamation and supported legislation to conserve natural resources, which won him the approval of Wyomingites. He said, "I know Wyoming and Wyoming people. I know their worth." Courtesy, Wyoming State Archives, Museums and Historical Department

Fenimore Chatterton to commute the sentence. Many people thought that Horn had employers who could not afford to let him hang, because he might name them in his last moments.

John Coble had supposedly hired Horn on behalf of the Wyoming Stockgrowers Association to stop cattle rustling, which had gotten out of hand. Except for his drunken boast, Horn never admitted to the Nickell murder, never named his employers, and accepted the hangman's noose calmly. He was hanged November 20, 1903, at the Laramie County jail in front of a large crowd of spectators. The question of his guilt or innocence is still debated by historians.

MUNICIPAL SERVICES

The 1880s saw Cheyenne become a modern city, possessing such municipal utilities as electricity, water service, telephone, street maintenance, public transportation, and police and fire protection. Street and alley maintenance had begun in 1874, with the purchase of a cart and mule and the hiring of a man for $25 per month or 40 cents per load of gravel.

In 1884 Cheyenne got its water supply from Lake Mahpaklutah, a mile and a half north of town. Now known as Sloan's Lake

Above: Cheyenne Post Office and Federal Building was constructed between 1898 and 1905. Interior walls were lined with pink and grey marble, doorways and trim were of polished hardwoods, and the stair railings and fixtures were brass. The exterior was grey Rawlins stone with granite entrances. After the government abandoned the building in 1965, no practical use could be found for it, so it was demolished within two years to make way for a bank building. Courtesy, Wyoming State Archives, Museums and Historical Department

Above: Percy Hoyt, right, was instrumental in the organization of a paid fire department in Cheyenne in 1909, and served as chief of the department for a time. Hoyt originally belonged to one of the volunteer fire groups. Courtesy, Wyoming State Archives, Museums and Historical Department

in Holliday Park, it is near the downtown area and well within the city limits. When there were fires, three volunteer fire departments responded to the ten-bell general alarm and the two-bell "fire-out" signals. In 1909 full-time salaried firemen replaced the volunteers.

A telephone exchange was established in Cheyenne in 1881, and connections were made to Laramie, Fort Russell, and Camp Carlin. By 1884 there were 145 telephones in Cheyenne. In 1911 phone lines were installed in the famous Plains Hotel during its construction.

These mule-drawn covered wagons on Ferguson (now Carey Avenue) in the early 1880s may have been supply wagons from Fort Russell. Rutted dirt streets and board sidewalks carried downtown traffic. A central power plant was built around this time, furnishing many of the downtown businesses with electricity. Courtesy, Wyoming State Archives, Museums and Historical Department

Cheyenne Gas Company began providing gas for lighting and heating in November 1883. One of the first commercial lighting plants in the West was Brush-Swan Electric Company of Cheyenne, formed in January 1883. Thirty downtown buildings were lighted by the first circuit, and in May streetlights were operating. To accommodate buildings wired for electricity but not located along the light company's circuits, wagons delivered storage batteries at dusk each day. In the morning the batteries were picked up and returned to the light plant for recharging. The light company furnished extra batteries for parties or special events.

By 1885 there were approximately 50 private households using electricity in Cheyenne. Carbon-fired arc lights were used at intersections; when the carbons were replaced weekly, neighborhood children scrambled to get the discarded carbon sticks, which they used for writing on fences and sidewalks.

Cheyenne Light, Fuel and Power Company, organized in 1900, bought out Brush-Swan. The company put up a steam-generating plant and installed street mains to carry steam to heat buildings on 16th Street, Cap-

itol Avenue, and Carey Avenue. In 1911 steam meters were installed for customers. By the 1950s and early 1960s the steam system had as many as 240 customers. However, about this time many old buildings using steam heat were demolished and replaced by buildings using natural gas. By 1977 the number of customers had declined to 63, and in July 1979 the steam heating system was abandoned. The three 140-foot stacks at the plant, long-time Cheyenne landmarks, were removed in June 1984.

Public transportation began in January 1888; the Cheyenne Street Railroad Company provided 30-passenger horse-drawn cars on a 30-minute schedule. There were three lines: a red-painted car served northwest Cheyenne and the fairgrounds, a yellow car served 19th Street east to Russell, and a green car served the capitol building and cemetery. After four years the unprofitable enterprise was terminated. In 1908 the Cheyenne Electric Railway was established, serving the Union Pacific depot, downtown and residential areas, Lake Minnehaha, and the new Frontier Park. It operated until 1924. In 1929 the Cheyenne Motor Bus Company began service in the city, which lasted until 1959. Cheyenne was then without public transportation until the Jitney mini-bus service began in 1982.

AUTOMOBILES
The New York-to-Paris automobile race passed through Cheyenne in 1908, awakening interest in this new mode of transportation. The 1909 legislature introduced a bill requiring owners to stop their machines on public roads in the presence of frightened

Below: Cheyenne Steam Laundry's teams lined up in front of the building, ready to load for deliveries. The five-bulb street lights were installed in 1911. In 1921 new single-light street lamps replaced the multiple lights. Courtesy, Wyoming State Archives, Museums and Historical Department

horses and to give their names and addresses to anyone on demand. The bill failed, but by 1913 a bill passed requiring "registration, identification, and regulation of automobiles" in Wyoming. Motor vehicle operators were also required to stop on signal until restive animals had passed.

In 1936 Wyoming issued its unique license plate with the bucking horse logo. This logo can also be seen in many other places throughout the state besides on vehicle plates—highway park signs, state property logos, university football helmets, tourist brochures—and as the First National Bank and Trust logo.

THE AIRPORT
In May 1920 the federal government established the Transcontinental Air Mail Service, and Cheyenne was selected as one of the 14 stops on the route. At first the airfield was no more than a cleared stretch of buffalo grass and a hangar, but after the hangar was destroyed by fire, the airport was rebuilt and enlarged. Four hangars and an administra-

tion building were dedicated in December 1925. These new facilities prompted the superintendent of the air service to declare Cheyenne's facility the best in the nation. Boeing Air Transport Company was authorized to carry both mail and passengers in 1927, and regular service was started from Cheyenne to Chicago and to California. Boeing, which became United Air Lines, operated its flight attendant school in Cheyenne until 1961.

During the 1930s the dirt-and-grass runways were replaced by asphalt; in 1942 the asphalt was replaced by concrete; and in 1960 a new terminal was constructed. Today the Wyoming Air National Guard is based at Cheyenne Airport.

HOSPITALS

Cheyenne has enjoyed hospital facilities since its inception. Laramie County Memorial Hospital has been in existence since 1867, growing as the need in the community has grown.

The Veterans Administration Hospital, constructed in 1934 as a medical and regional office center for the Veterans Administration, provides medical attention to approximately 2,000 veterans annually. In addition, 73,000 veterans and dependents contact the center annually for benefits information.

Depaul Hospital, the first and only Catholic hospital in Wyoming, opened in July 1952. An expansion project, begun in 1974, brought it up to par with modern hospitals. Depaul's Home Health Program was

Below: The advent of motor cars allowed Cheyenne residents to go on outings to such places as Granite Springs Reservoir, about 25 miles west of Cheyenne. The little girl in the front of the boat is the granddaughter of the photographer, J.E. Stimson. Stimson took thousands of pictures of the area around the turn of the century. Courtesy, Wyoming State Archives, Museums and Historical Department

Above: In July 1911 the Kirkbride wedding party struck a serious pose in a chain-driven horseless carriage. Today the Kirkbride's ranch, east of Cheyenne, is the site of one of the Minuteman missiles. Courtesy, Wyoming State Archives, Museums and Historical Department

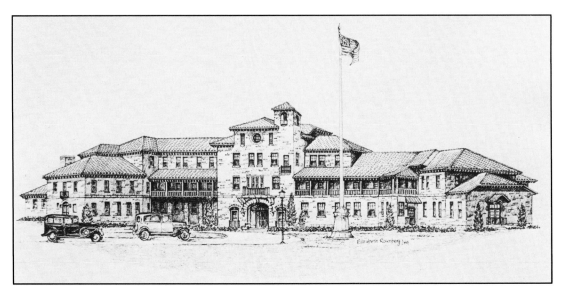

launched in 1975, and Frontier Hospice, providing support for home care of the terminally ill, began in 1981. Depaul also has a chemical dependency center, and it is the location of Wyoming's poison control center.

BANKING

Banking began in Cheyenne in September 1867 when H.J. Rogers opened a bank in the Cornforth Brothers Store. Shortly after that, two Denver-affiliated banks were located at Kountz Brothers and Company and J.A. Ware and Company.

By 1888, when the territorial legislature passed a state banking act, there were five banks in Cheyenne: First National, Cheyenne National, Stockgrowers National, and two private banks owned by T.A. Kent and Morton E. Post. One of the most enduring banks, Stockgrowers National, was founded by five investors: Joseph Carey and his brother Davis, Thomas Sturges and his brother William, and Henry Hay. These men, who would all become influential in Cheyenne, felt that the area provided excellent investment potential because of the booming cattle business—in which all five were engaged—and the stability provided by Fort D.A. Russell and the Union Pacific Railroad.

In 1905 a new building was constructed for the Stockgrowers bank at the corner of

Top: The Veterans Administration Hospital, now surrounded by residential and commercial developments, was built in 1934 on a 600-acre cow pasture, at a cost of $750,000. The property boasts 11,000 trees, which help it retain its original country flavor. This drawing by Elizabeth Rosenberg depicts the building as it looked just after construction.

Bottom: Wyoming Governor Nellie Tayloe Ross dug the first shovelful of dirt for new hangars at Cheyenne Airport in 1925. At that time, in spite of its dirt and grass runways, Cheyenne's facility was the best in the United States, according to the National Air Service. Courtesy, Wyoming State Archives, Museums and Historical Department

17th Street and Capitol Avenue. The bank remains at that site, having undergone several remodelings and a name change: in 1964 it became the First National Bank and Trust of Wyoming.

WYOMING STOCKGROWERS ASSOCIATION

The Wyoming Stockgrowers Association has been influential in the state since its organization in April 1871. Its membership is headed by an executive committee, with representatives from all counties. Governor John A. Campbell served as the association's first president. The stated purpose of the organization was the "advancement of cattle and sheep growing" in the territory. The association administered a "general fund to be expended in the detection, arrest, and conviction of stock thieves, and in the purchase of rope with which to hang them."

The Wyoming Stockgrowers Association's first meeting in November 1871 was a spectacular success. The Union Pacific provided half-fare rates and the state house of representatives joined the stockraisers for their meeting. Soon after, the legislature passed a law against livestock theft, authorizing punishment of up to 10 years in prison

This majestic building, built in 1907-1908, still stands in downtown Cheyenne. Originally it housed the First National Bank, founded by Amasa Converse of Converse and Warren Mercantile. This bank was not the predecessor of the present National Bank and Trust in Cheyenne; it went broke in 1924. The Capitol Theater, on the left, was built in 1902 for live theater; it was rebuilt in 1917 as Paramount Movie Theater. Courtesy, Wyoming State Archives, Museums and Historical Department

and a $5,000 fine. It also authorized fines up to $500 and five years in prison for altering brands.

These measures did not decrease the number of thefts, however, and convictions were virtually impossible to obtain. The organization declined in the 1870s and reorganized later as a cattlemen's association; by this time the sheepmen and the cattlemen were at each other's throats.

The Stockgrowers Association was quite large and powerful at one time, inspiring passage of a law that required registration of brands benefiting cattlemen. This power slackened in subsequent years, and the association has suffered its ups and downs, but it remains influential in the state, with Cheyenne as its headquarters.

Times of Trouble for Cheyenne

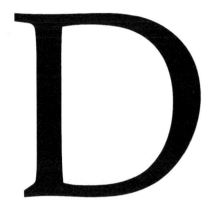

Disasters and tragedies are a part of growth, and Cheyenne has experienced its share in the form of floods, droughts, blizzards, and a tornado. Because of its climate and geography—high winds and treeless plains—the area is conducive to blizzards and flooding. Man has also contributed to problems in the area by allowing overgrazing of the land, which is especially disastrous when coupled with cycles of drought and flooding. Fires have brought their share of destruction to the growing city as well.

Most of Cheyenne's downtown business section was destroyed by fire in 1870. Two city blocks burned, destroying dozens of businesses that were housed in the hastily built, ramshackle structures of the time. Joslins and Park Jewelers, occupying a stone-and-mortar building on the southeast corner of 16th Street and Carey Avenue, survived the fire, proving the worth of substantial structures. The fire raged around it, demolishing most of the surrounding two blocks.

In an effort to save at least the furniture and fixtures, people in the newspaper office carried as much as they could out in the street, but the fire jumped from the building to the pile of furniture, and then continued across the street.

Many people speculated that Cheyenne was gone forever. However, a bird's-eye view of Cheyenne later in 1870 shows three-quarters of the business district already rebuilt. The remainder was rebuilt during 1871 and 1872. Cheyenne passed a fire code as a result of the disaster, requiring that subsequent buildings be constructed of brick or stone or be "iron clad." Fire struck again in January 1873 and July 1874—presumably set

Facing page: In the aftermath of this spring snowstorm in 1920, it must have been hard to believe that Cheyenne enjoys an average of 235 sunny days each year. Springtime rains often come in the form of snow, but usually melt away within a day or two. Courtesy, Wyoming State Archives, Museums and Historical Department

When Crow Creek could no longer retain within its banks the accumulated water from spring rains and mountain snow melt, the lowland areas of Cheyenne were flooded, as seen in this 1896 photograph. Until the creek was deepened this was a common early summer occurrence. Courtesy, Wyoming State Archives, Museums and Historical Department

by Indians as a diversion so that they could release a prisoner from jail—and on other occasions, but it never again caused such extensive damage.

A different type of "disaster" took place on July 2, 1885, when that year's Independence Day celebration started off with a 10,000-pound firecracker—formerly a powder storage house. It had been built of stone, which fragments when it explodes, and had a peak roof, which gathered heat from the sun. The structure was vented to let the heat out through only a central tower. In short, the powder storage house was designed like a hand grenade. The July heat attracted lightning, causing an explosion that blew stones for two miles, broke a horse's leg, and blew the heads off several chickens within the bombardment area. It wasn't a very big disaster for Cheyenne, but it was certainly a well-timed spectacle.

FLOODS

Flooding occurred at regular intervals, especially in the days before flood-control measures were taken. During most of the year, Crow Creek appeared a shallow, slow-running stream meandering through the plains; however, spring rains, a sudden cloudburst, or quick snowmelt in the mountains transformed it into a swollen, unstoppable, ever-widening river engulfing everything in its path.

Floods occurred in 1879, 1891, and 1896, but the most memorable one took place in 1904. The May 20, 1904, flood began with a

cloudburst 12 miles upstream from Cheyenne and flooded many homes in the lowland areas of the town. Around 16th Street and Snyder, Dillon, and Ames, several homes were washed off their sites by the water. Two children were drowned in their bed in a house at 15th and Snyder. Another flood occurred in June 1929 because of heavy showers near the headwaters of the creek, where the ground was already saturated and tributaries were full from the melting of heavy snows.

Crow Creek was eventually straightened and deepened, and attempts were made to beautify and preserve as open space the floodplain along the waterway. Two Cheyenne businessmen, William C. Deming and George Brimmer, retained, at their own expense, the noted designer of Denver parks, S.R. DeBoer, to create plans for a scenic drive that would emphasize the assets of the creek as well as eliminate the hazards. Deming was publisher of the *Wyoming State Tribune* at the time, and Brimmer a prominent attorney. Deming left money in his will to be used for the extension, construction, and landscaping of Deming Drive along Crow Creek. His hope was that the drive would be extended southeast to Archer, east of Cheyenne, and north to Hynds Boulevard, "making an attractive suburban drive."

Flooding did not disappear, however, with the improvement of Crow Creek. Water dangers extend even into modern times. On August 1, 1985, Cheyenne experienced the

Bottom: Cheyenne residents survey the flooded civic center parking lot on the morning after the storm August 1, 1985. Cheyenne experienced six inches of rainfall and inches of hail that evening, within four hours time.
Photo by Mark Junge

Top: Snowplows piled up banks of hail the morning after the devastating August 1, 1985 storm. Photo by Mark Junge

deadliest flood in its history. That evening a sudden thunderstorm dumped six inches of rain and another six inches of marble-sized hail on the town within four hours' time on ground that had already absorbed two inches of rain during the past week and in an area that normally experiences 12 to 13 inches of precipitation annually.

Normally dry, Crow and Dry creeks overflowed their banks, leaving four feet of water standing in parts of town. Homes and businesses flooded, forcing people out. Several families who had taken refuge in their basements in response to a tornado sighting barely managed to escape in time as hail broke windows and rain rushed in, flooding their basements.

Seventy-three year old Alice Paulson drowned in her basement, where she had gone to escape the tornado. Although three tornadoes were reported, none caused damage. The water did that. A total of 12 people were killed, most by drowning, as cars were swept from streets into Crow and Dry creeks. Ironically, Dry Creek flooded the same neighborhoods that were hit by the tornado of 1979.

Sheriff's Deputy Robert Van Alyne tied himself to a telephone pole in order to pull three people from a partially submerged car. After he got two people out, he returned to the car for a little girl. They were both washed away by the floodwaters and numbered among the victims.

During the storm, wind gusts reached 70 miles per hour, and lightning was almost continuous. After the storm abated, National Guard trucks evacuated people from their flooded homes to shelters. One young woman recalls being plucked through her living room window by a guardsman while the rising water held her front door shut.

Insurance company representatives estimated $28 million in property and auto damage. That estimate didn't include the flood-damaged homes that were not covered by flood insurance. Only 130 Cheyenne homes were insured for flood.

Two days after the storm, flood victims, neighbors, National Guard and Air Force personnel worked to bail water and shovel away the muck piled inside homes and buildings, and outside on yards, streets, and sidewalks. Cheyenne was repairing and rebuilding.

BLIZZARDS

The winter of 1886-1887 has become legendary in the West. The summer had been dry, so grass was sparse and the cattle were thin and in poor condition. Winter came early. October was a month of heavy snows that did not melt, December brought many blizzards, and January was even worse, with gale winds and never-ending snow. Temperatures were below zero even during the day, and at night they dropped to 40 and 50 degrees below. A number of ranch employees were found frozen to death on the range, and trains stalled on the tracks. By spring, carcasses of dead cattle were strewn along draws and streams from Canada down through Montana, Wyoming, and Colorado. Tens of thousands of cattle and sheep on the range had perished. Hundreds of buzzards appeared in the country to feast on the carrion. They were not known before in Wyoming, nor have they been seen since. After that terrible winter, in the late 1880s, Wyoming experienced a state-wide depression because of cattle losses brought about by overgrazing and drought, as well as the extremes of weather. Many of Cheyenne's cattle barons lost their investments and returned to Europe; others struggled for years to recoup their losses.

The blizzard of 1949 was remembered by a succeeding generation as the worst blizzard of a lifetime: six weeks of cold, snow, wind, and heroic efforts. Ranchers, railroaders, and travelers were caught in the blizzard, and some perished. Snowdrifts were 20 to 50 feet high and 50- to 80-mile-per-hour winds whipped the area day after day. When planes could finally get off the ground, they began airlifting food, medicine, and hay, and conducted rescue missions. Automobile owners who left their stalled vehicles returned after the wind died down to find them drifted over and sometimes buried; digging out became a two or three day job.

In his memoirs, *I Remember,* Con Hansen wrote:

On a barren hillside near the Wheatland road about three miles from Highway 30 stood a lonely dead yearling steer. With nose to the

Top: During the 1949 blizzard in Cheyenne, many roads were plowed out through deep drifts of snow which sometimes nearly reached the height of the power lines. Courtesy, Wyoming State Archives, Museums and Historical Department

Bottom: This ranch house at Lusk, a small community approximately 30 miles northeast of Cheyenne, was snowed in during the winter of 1949. Courtesy, Wyoming State Archives, Museums and Historical Department

ground and feet spread apart he stood there, a grim and horrible reminder of the severity of the blizzard just passed . . . Every day I noticed him . . . one day I stopped . . . to have a closer look. It was frozen hard as iron, so well braced or frozen down that I couldn't push it over. The hair was packed full of hard snow and the eyes were only blobs of snow and ice. There it remained standing for several weeks, until a few warm days should thaw the joints enough for it to settle down to the ground in an upright position.

Not all stories connected with the blizzard were grim. The following story got national play on wire services and later appeared in *Readers' Digest:*

A long-time resident retrieved from mothballs an ancient bearskin coat which he reasoned would provide maximum protection from the blowing snow. As he drove over a lonely country road,

his automobile stalled. He was forced to make his way over an open, snow-covered field to a ranch house. As he moved across the field, an Operation Haylift pilot spotted the fur-clad figure from above and dropped a bale of hay practically at his feet.

In the winter of 1978-1979 Wyoming and Cheyenne again experienced the worst blizzard in years. That winter, as in other blizzard winters, animals died, ranchers were isolated, hay was airlifted to stranded cattle, and water lines froze. There were long stretches of below-zero weather; in some parts of the state, the thermometer remained below freezing for months. Damage to wildlife, homes, and livestock was estimated at $10 million. The losses included 2,000 cattle, 13,000 calves, 2,760 sheep, and 20,000 lambs.

Although ranchers have developed different techniques for wintering their stock, resulting in higher survival rates during bad weather, the wind, snow, and blizzards will remain a difficult part of life in and around Cheyenne.

DECLINE OF THE RAILROAD

Union Pacific Railroad President Charles Francis Adams announced in January 1889 that the central repair shops for the entire

During World War I, women were temporarily employed in the Union Pacific freight-yards, until after the armistice when men again filled those positions. The Equality State believed in women voting, but not working "men's jobs." Courtesy, Wyoming State Archives, Museums and Historical Department

Union Pacific system would be located at Cheyenne. This was expected to provide relief to the local economy, which had suffered serious setbacks due to the decline of the livestock industry. Developers and speculators invested new money in Cheyenne—a housing development called Interior Heights was proposed south of town, and a normal college was planned—but within three years the international financial panic of 1893 struck. The Union Pacific was severely affected, and Cheyenne's growth was halted until the war years, when both Cheyenne and the railroad joined the rest of the country in prosperity brought about by international conflict. However, the new boom was short-lived. The nationwide decline of railroads in the 1940s after the transportation takeover by automobiles had a tremendous impact on Cheyenne; after the cattle bust, the Union Pacific had become the largest industry in Cheyenne.

WAR, PROHIBITION, DEPRESSION, AND DROUGHT

The United States entered the "war to end all wars," World War I, in April 1917. In Cheyenne, as in other parts of the country, wartime activities brought prosperity. Two regiments of cavalry were stationed at Fort

D.A. Russell. Various church groups staged fund-raisers for war relief and entertainment for the military; housewives prepared bandages and knitted articles for servicemen.

Late in the war, a national epidemic of Spanish influenza was responsible for more deaths than the war itself. Throughout Wyoming, public meetings were banned and churches and schools were closed. In Cheyenne, stores that remained open were limited to five customers at one time for each 25 feet of store front.

After the war, on July 1, 1919, the Wyoming legislature passed a prohibition bill and the state went dry by law, although not in fact. A last fling, the night before passage of the bill, was described as one of the wildest in Cheyenne's history. *The Wyoming State Tribune* said: "The melancholy days have come ... Cheyenne awoke this morning with a headache, a yearning thirst, a fuzzy taste in its mouth, and not a chance for the morning eye-opener." Not everyone went thirsty, though, for those who could afford it had stocked their private cellars. According to official policy, private stores would not be molested by officers of the law; sometimes hijackers invaded well-stocked cellars, however. Individuals soon began brewing their own liquor with private stills, and some small ranchers sold it in an effort to make ends meet during the post-war deflation and the Depression years.

After one year of Prohibition, the *Wyoming State Tribune* reported that anyone who wanted a drink could find it: "First there is old stuff that has been kept but costs a small fortune, then there is the home-made brew, and then comes perfume, hair tonic, flavoring extracts and patent medicines . . . these produce some peculiar results and make some men wild." After the repeal of Prohibition in 1933, the Wyoming legislature established a state liquor commission, which was to engage in liquor wholesaling as a source of revenue.

In this arid region of the country, drought is one of nature's cruelest weapons. Because of severe drought in 1919, one-third of Wyoming's cattle had to be shipped either to market or to out-of-state pastures. Even the antelope sought grass elsewhere. A moratorium on hunting antelope remained in effect until 1925.

In January 1923 the Union Pacific established a freight terminal at Cheyenne, to be a distribution point for Wyoming and adjoining states. This project involved expansion of the existing yards, the building of a new freight terminal, construction of a new steel-and-concrete viaduct, improvement of the city's water system, and construction of housing for railroad employees. Many in Cheyenne were hopeful, but the terminal did not stave off the Depression. The state of Wyoming experienced hard times years ahead of the rest of the country, beginning in the early 1920s. Three of Cheyenne's leading banks were closed in July 1924.

Drought, with its resulting crop failures and the downtrend of the cattle industry, postwar deflation and the nationwide depression, declining oil and coal business, Union Pacific layoffs, national coal strikes, and bank failures—all contributed to the plunge of Cheyenne, along with Wyoming and the rest of the country, into the Great Depression.

Drought again compounded Wyoming's distress in 1933, 1934, and 1936. Government assistance became necessary for the majority of residents: the Civilian Conservation Corps put many young men to work, and the federal Public Works Administration put up many buildings, including the Wyoming Supreme Court building in Cheyenne. An indigent transients' camp in Cheyenne required residents to work for their room and board.

WAR AGAIN

The United States declaration of war, following the December 7, 1941, attack on Pearl Harbor, galvanized Wyoming to patriotism. Because Fort Francis E. Warren, formerly Fort Russell, was almost filled to capacity by a garrison of 3,500 officers and men, new construction was initiated to expand the facilities. Wyoming also had an army air base near Casper, a prisoner of war camp near Douglas, and a Japanese relocation center between Cody and Powell.

During 1942 and 1943, more than 20,000 men were regularly stationed at Fort Warren. The economic impact of the fort on Cheyenne was enormous. Despite shortages, the standard of living rose during wartime. Cheyenne had a USO, and the young soldiers on leave danced and socialized in town. Movies also became very popular among soldiers as well as civilians.

Second to Fort Warren, agriculture was the largest business in the state. Production of livestock and crops accelerated, and many farmers and ranchers were able to pay off accumulated debts. Other industries increased their output as well, so that after the war Wyoming was in solid financial condition.

In the 1950s Wyoming's already sparse population was diminishing, partly because many young people left the state for jobs. However, in 1947, when Fort Warren became Warren Air Force Base, the increased activity and manpower at the base made a positive contribution to Cheyenne's economy and

Left: The first officially reported tornado in Cheyenne's history ripped out a path of destruction on the afternoon of July 16, 1979. In 25 minutes it was all over. Although 57 were injured, only one person was killed. Courtesy, Wyoming State Archives, Museums and Historical Department

Right: Meteorologists called Cheyenne's tornado of July 16, 1979, the largest, most destructive such storm in Wyoming history. The low number of casualties was called a miracle. Courtesy, Wyoming State Archives, Museums and Historical Department

social life and the civic involvement of its people. In the 1970s the economy of Wyoming was further boosted by the production of oil, as one of the state's 14 oil refineries was established in Cheyenne. Thus, the town began to regain its financial footing.

TORNADO!

In the mid-afternoon of July 16, 1979, a tornado touched down in Buffalo Ridge, a northwestern subdivision of Cheyenne, and created a three-mile long path of destruction, leveling 140 homes and damaging 250 others in 25 minutes. A thousand people were left homeless, 57 injured, and one 14-month-old boy was killed. His mother was so seriously injured that she died within the year.

Top: A homeowner assessed the damage from his former second-floor bedroom after the 1979 tornado. Within two hours of the devastation, a Warren Air Force Base helicopter had surveyed the damage, and the base provided barricades for traffic control, portable generators, ambulances, medical supplies, and technicians. Courtesy, F.E. Warren Air Force Base

Bottom: Once a surburban home, this pile of rubbish awaited the cleanup crews after the 1979 tornado. President Jimmy Carter declared Cheyenne a major disaster area, and a formal request for cleanup support resulted in Warren Air Force Base personnel and equipment for a three-day cleaning effort. Courtesy, F.E. Warren Air Force Base

Base personnel provided strong backs and ready hands as well as equipment to assist the people of Cheyenne in the massive cleanup and recovery after the first tornado in the city's history. Courtesy, F.E. Warren Air Force Base

The tornado was erratic in its destruction: a collection of mobile homes became a pile of tangled debris; the walls of a house stood, although the roof had disappeared; nothing remained of another home but its foundation and basement; a pile of lumber and debris lay where another house once stood; a car was neatly parked but its garage was gone; another car was upside down in a backyard; a two-by-four stuck through a wall like a dart; chain link fences were twisted beyond salvage; and power lines were down.

A newspaper story reported: "An eyewitness, father of four children, described the storm: 'You can't believe the roar that thing made. At first I thought it was an explosion.' The family hid in the basement, listening to the force of the twister as it chewed homes to bits, expecting any moment to hear their own house being ripped apart above them."

Cleanup began immediately. Residents, friends, and Warren Air Force Base personnel were out in the streets picking up debris and collecting blankets, clothing, food, and medical supplies for the victims.

The annual Frontier Days celebration had been scheduled to begin the following Saturday, on July 21. Cheyenne Mayor Don Erickson stated in the press, "Frontier Days will be held. The community will continue its business. We are a hardy group here in Cheyenne, you know. People will all pitch in and help out." By the time the annual rodeo began, the only evidence of the tragedy were the ruins of buildings that were in the tornado's path. As a result of this unpredicted disaster, a siren warning system was put into effect, and tornado watches are broadcast over the local radio stations. Western fortitude has prevailed in Cheyenne since 1867, and it will probably continue to prevail.

CHAPTER VI

Cheyenne Looks to Its Present and Future

Cheyenne's early days epitomized action. The "Magic City of the Plains" sprang into full-fledged existence in a single day. Modern civilization and permanent settlers arrived by train; buildings arrived by sections on railroad cars. Because the settlers were sophisticated businessmen, attitudes of commercialism and political conservatism dominated. Cheyenne and Wyoming remain conservative to this day.

While many other railroad terminal towns floundered or completely disappeared when the railroad moved on, the "Magic City" continued to grow and prosper. In 1895, with a population of 11,000, Cheyenne was the wealthiest city per capita in the nation.

Cheyenne's industrial base has changed in the course of its history. Cattle, sheep, agriculture, minerals, and the railroad all still have their place in the local economy. Cheyenne is a governmental center for the city, county, and state, and many federal offices are based there. Warren Air Force Base also has a large impact on the area.

Tourism has come into its own in Wyoming and is becoming more important in Cheyenne. It is easy to get to Cheyenne, because two interstate highways—I-25 north/south and I-80 east/west—intersect southwest of the city. Frontier Days draws thousands of visitors each summer, and many of them are pleased and surprised to discover the richness of Cheyenne's heritage.

Many of Cheyenne's 50,000 citizens are interested in the preservation and appreciation of their city's past. Many historic homes and buildings have been preserved and refurbished. These buildings are often used

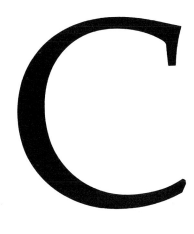

Facing page: The Tivoli building, at 16th Street and Carey Avenue, is now occupied by the Greater Cheyenne Chamber of Commerce after extensive reconstruction. It was originally built by the Richardson brothers in 1892 as a restaurant and bar to replace their previous cafe that was in operation at least as early as 1887. Old reports claim that a tunnel connected the Tivoli with other downtown buildings so the "city fathers" could visit the rathskeller, and the upstairs, in privacy. Cheyenne women could take tea there most afternoons, and listen to the latest modern mechanical piano. Photo by Jim Birrell

as professional offices or association head-quarters, and some offer tours of their premises to the public.

THE RAINSFORD DISTRICT

A historic neighborhood known as the Rainsford District, constructed between 1880 and 1930, is bounded, roughly, by Warren and Morrie avenues, and by 16th and 25th streets. Within these boundaries are the homes of Daze Bristol, the "First Lady of Frontier

Top: A roof sign advertises Frontier Days, and bunting decorates buildings along the parade route, in this photograph taken from the Union Pacific depot looking north up Capitol Avenue in the late 1920s. Courtesy, Wyoming State Archives, Museums and Historical Department

Bottom: Capitol Avenue looks the same today as it did in 1984 when this picture was taken, except for the addition of new state and federal government buildings near the state capitol. Photo by Jim Birrell

Facing page: Completed and occupied in 1984, the new Herschler State Office Building was designed to complement the state capitol building. Located directly north of and adjacent to the capitol, it was limited to four stories, making it as tall as the capitol's wings but shorter than the capitol's gold dome, a city landmark.
Photo by Jim Birrell

Days"; architect George D. Rainsford; the historic governor's mansion; the Crook house, the home of the first permanent physician in Cheyenne and the best example of Queen Anne architecture in the city; the Samuel Corson home, still owned by his descendants; the Warren-Nagle mansion, now the YWCA; the home of Nellie Tayloe Ross, the first female governor in the country; the home of suffragette Esther Hobart Morris, and others. The neighborhood takes its name from George D. Rainsford, an eccentric New York architect who came to Wyoming in the late 1870s and started the Diamond Ranch near Chugwater. Eventually Rainsford built a home in Cheyenne and pursued architecture as a hobby. He designed many of the homes in the district, including several on 17th and 18th streets, known as "Baron's Row" because of the many mansions erected there by wealthy cattle ranchers in the 1800s.

Another area of downtown Cheyenne, from Carey and Capitol avenues north of the capitol building to Frontier Park, came to be known as "Millionaire's Row." This area, containing many large properties, has been well-maintained throughout the years. Many of the homes there were built more recently than those in the Rainsford District.

Above: The "new" governor's mansion was first occupied in October 1976 when Governor and Mrs. Ed Herschler moved from the historic residence on East 21st Street which had served since 1905. In contrast to the formality of the historic mansion, the landscaping, architecture, and decor of the new residence combine to create a feeling of western warmth and informality. Photo by Jim Birrell

Below: Flags flying over the Cheyenne Frontier Days' Old West Museum in Frontier Park welcome natives and visitors to an exhaustive collection of early West memorabilia. To the right of the U.S. flag is Wyoming's state flag, and the flag on the left proclaims Cheyenne Frontier Days the "Daddy of 'em All." Photo by Judith Adams

Facing page: Twin viaducts spanning the railroad yards from 16th Street to I-80 opened in July 1982 and June 1984. They are equipped with geothermal systems on their northern approaches. Some 4,000 tons of steel, costing about four million dollars, were used in their construction. The original Riner viaduct, an all-wood structure built in 1892, was named after J.S. Riner, mayor of Cheyenne from 1887 to 1891. It was replaced by a steel structure in 1929 in a joint venture of the Union Pacific Railroad, Laramie County, and the federal government. Courtesy, Wyoming State Highway Department

Top: Substantial homes, dirt streets, and no trees created a rural atmosphere right on the edge of the city in 1910. Courtesy, Mr. and Mrs. Julian Carpender

Bottom: This 1975 scene, looking north from the capitol dome, was that of a typical small city residential area. Courtesy, Wyoming State Highway Department

The neighborhood remains a desirable location within the city.

THE RETAIL ECONOMY

As is now typical for virtually every American city, the new mall northeast of town has affected Cheyenne's downtown retail area. The chamber of commerce, with the support of local merchants, has become interested in the revitalization of the heart of Cheyenne. The Downtown Development Authority has been organized and is presently studying various ideas, plans, and architectural proposals designed to reinstate the historical character of the 1800s while incorporating new buildings.

Early on, Cheyenne was known as the "cultural center of the West," boasting the only opera house west of the Mississippi. Today it is home to the "Daddy of 'Em All," the biggest and best-known rodeo in the world. Cultural events have remained important in Cheyenne: Little Theatre Players has been known as one of the best theatrical groups in the Rocky Mountain area since 1929. A great number of music, art, and literary groups also exists in the city.

A new civic center, erected in 1980-1981, houses the Cheyenne Symphony and Choral Society, which was established in 1954 with volunteer musicians from the community. In 1981 the orchestra became professional, with paid musicians and a professional music director/conductor, and it provides an annual series of high-quality symphony performances.

In contrast to Cheyenne's early citizens, who lived during the days of fast action, today's residents are unhurried, friendly, and straightforward. Community involvement is an integral part of life. High school homecoming parades down Capitol Avenue on Friday afternoons in October bring shopkeepers and office workers out of their buildings to shout encouragement to cheerleaders and ballplayers.

Among today's Cheyenne residents, the most popular vehicle is a pickup truck, preferably one with four-wheel drive. A pickup is not only a status symbol but is also the most useful vehicle one can own. Some are equipped with snowplows and winches, indicating the self-reliant attitude so prevalent in Cheyenne.

Since its beginnings, Cheyenne has had a special rapport with Fort Russell and later Warren Air Force Base; base personnel have become closely involved in community affairs. Former Air Force Secretary Hans M. March once commented, "The relationship between the base and the community here is one of the best in the country."

Those who live in and around Cheyenne enjoy the quality of life it offers. High and dry at an elevation of 6,000 feet, Cheyenne is blessed with blue skies and sunshine an average of 235 days annually, and frequent winds keep the air fresh and clean. Summer temperatures seldom reach 90 degrees, and the nights are cool. Winter days are often sunny, with temperatures as high as 40 degrees. Nights are cold, with temperatures sometimes dipping below zero. Snow usually melts quickly, but storms and blizzards do occur often enough to give the area an "icebox" reputation. Most of the snow occurs during late winter and early spring; a white Christmas is less likely than a white Easter.

Above: Daze Bristol, known as the "First Lady of Frontier Days," selected and trained dancers for her dance hall float for more than 40 years. She also wrote columns for the Cheyenne newspapers and Stockman Farmer for 37 years. She lived in the house her husband built in 1904 until her death in 1983 at the age of 105. Daze was an institution in Cheyenne. Courtesy, Wyoming State Archives, Museums and Historical Department

Below: When formal Frontier Days parades were initiated, Daze Bristol designed a number of floats—Dazee's Dancers, Hell's Half Acre, Silver Crown Mining, Placer Mining, The Blacksmith, and Vigilantes— which still appear in the parades today. For many years Daze played the organ on this dance hall float, seen here, surrounded by the dancers and other musicians. Courtesy, Wyoming State Archives, Museums and Historical Department

Vedauwoo, 37 miles west of Cheyenne, has been a favorite camping and picnic area since the advent of the automobile. Vedauwoo is an Indian word meaning "earth born." The area was once a tribal camping ground. Courtesy, Wyoming Travel Commission

The countryside might appear barren to someone driving in and around Cheyenne, but on foot the hiker sees a different world: ravines and gorges to traverse, numerous wildflowers, and grasses of different hues, from the blue sage to the dark green buffalo grass, which is highly nutritious for pastured cattle and horses. Wildlife is also abundant: herds of antelope and deer, hawks soaring over bluffs or outcroppings of rock, meadowlarks perched on fenceposts, more readily heard than seen, killdeer playing their games in fields, and gulls swooping above.

Fifty miles to the west are the Snowy Range Mountains, part of the Rocky Mountain chain. Known as an outdoorsman's paradise, the state of Wyoming is even more a photographer's ideal.

And so Cheyenne, with the same confidence and self-assurance that have forged its past, with its heritage strongly influencing its present, proudly faces its future.

The windswept prairie, dotted with bales of hay, is crowned by a rainbow on the horizon. Photo by Mark E. Gibson

Right: This large oil painting used to hang in the famous Cheyenne Club. Cattleman John Coble was forced to resign from the club after shooting holes in the painting with his .45. He explained that he shot "that Holstein bull" because it didn't look like any critter on his spread. Courtesy, Wyoming State Archives, Museums and Historical Department

Below: High-speed chuckwagon races, complete with four-horse teams and quick drivers, are a favorite event at Cheyenne's Frontier Days. Photo by Jim Messineo

Above: Parades are an integral part of Cheyenne's Frontier Days. More than 110,000 spectators line the downtown streets for the four parades during the ten-day celebration. Nearly 2,500 volunteers plan the annual event. Courtesy, Wyoming Travel Commission

Left: Calf-roping requires skill, expertise, and timing between horse and horseman. Courtesy, Wyoming Travel Commission

Right: Max Idelman built his luxurious mansion on Ferguson Street (later Carey Avenue) in the 1880s at a cost of $55,000. The home featured fireplaces in every bedroom, a ballroom, oak paneling, and treasures from the Idelmans' worldwide travels. Watercolor by Carleen Williams

Below: This home, at 2220 Capitol Avenue, belonged to Warren Richardson, who became a millionaire in the Salt Creek oil fields in Casper. He established Cheyenne's first newspaper, The Cheyenne Daily Leader. *Courtesy, Wyoming State Archives, Museums and Historical Department*

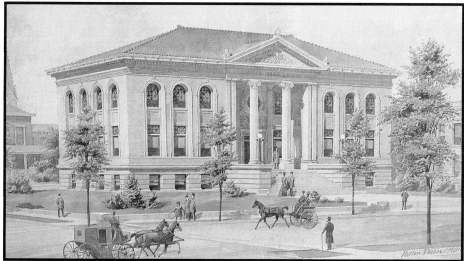

Above: The L.R. Bresnahen home, built in 1882 by wealthy cattleman William C. Irvine, was originally wired for electricity generated by batteries that had to be recharged frequently. When a central power plant was built in Cheyenne, this house was the first to be connected. Courtesy, Cheyenne Frontier Days Old West

Left: Although it was designed by a Chicago firm, the Carnegie Library was built by William Dubois of Cheyenne. It was the first county library to be established in the United States and was dedicated on February 5, 1902. Courtesy, Laramie County Library System

Facing page: The capitol building was con-structed in 1887 of sandstone from Fort Collins and Rawlins. In the French Renais-sance style, the building resembles the Hotel des Invalides of Paris. A parade, speeches, music, and a barbecue greeted its opening on May 18, 1887.
Photo by Jim Birrell

Above: The 1901 Wyoming Legislature authorized the building of this historic gover-nor's mansion, and appropriated $40,000 for that purpose. Under architect Charles W. Murdock, the Georgian-style building was completed late in 1904 at a total cost of $32,253.29. It served as the home of Wyoming's First Families until 1976 when a new governor's mansion was built. The orig-inal mansion was designated a National Historic site, and is open to the public.
Photo by Jim Birrell

Partners in Progress

I n Cheyenne, as in many American communities, business and industry has had its ever-important influence on local history.

There, the railroads started it—Cheyenne came into existence as a railroad terminus. Along with the railroad came the Army installations, growing from Fort Russell to Warren Air Force Base.

The raising of cattle followed. Foreign and domestic investors took advantage, not only of the highly nutritious grasses growing throughout the area, but also of the easy availability of transportation via railroads.

Located as it is on the high plains, Cheyenne has suffered the impact of nature in the form of high winds, heavy snows, and seasonal lack of water, resulting in devastation from blizzards, drought, and floods.

Underlying the changes, the peaks and valleys of Cheyenne's economy, is the attitude of individualism and frontier spirit that pervades Cheyenne's history—and promises to extend into its future.

The organizations whose stories are detailed on the following pages have chosen to support this important literary and civic project. They illustrate the variety of ways in which individuals and their businesses have contributed to the city's growth and development. The civic involvement of Cheyenne's businesses, institutions of learning, and local government, in cooperation with its citizens, has made the community an excellent place to live and work.

Facing page: This circa 1867 photograph depicts a construction outfit, typical of those working to put the railroad through at Crow Creek Crossing as well as at every other terminus along the route. Courtesy, Wyoming State Archives, Museums and Historical Department

GREATER CHEYENNE CHAMBER OF COMMERCE

The Tivoli building, at 16th and Carey, houses the Greater Cheyenne Chamber of Commerce. Established in 1892 by the Richardson brothers, it was originally a fine bar and restaurant, serving daily afternoon teas for ladies accompanied by organ music. A popular rathskeller was located in the basement.

Early in December 1906 a group of prominent citizens and businessmen met to discuss the organization of a commercial club in Cheyenne. As a result of that meeting, the Industrial Club of Cheyenne was formed in January 1907.

In 1910, 1911, and 1912 the club nominated members for the mayor to appoint to a committee called the Frontier Days Council. In either 1912 or 1913 the Industrial Club assumed full control of the Frontier Days Council, including its finances, conduct of the rodeo, publicity and promotion, and appointment of committee members.

At the annual meeting of the Industrial Club of Cheyenne on January 20, 1920, the name was changed to Cheyenne Chamber of Commerce and it incorporated two years later.

In August 1936 the chamber entered into an agreement with the City of Cheyenne, giving exclusive right and privilege of using Frontier Park "for the purpose of exhibiting therein the annual Frontier Days Celebration."

In 1966 the official name of the volunteer organization became Greater Cheyenne Chamber of Commerce.

The years 1967, 1970, and 1971 saw the chamber concentrating on economic development with the opening of Cannon Aeronautical Center, a modern new Husky Oil Refinery, and other efforts to bring industry and jobs into Cheyenne.

Education was another important task the chamber undertook in 1968 with the establishment of Laramie County Community College, and then again in 1979 with a $6.8-million expansion.

A positive move to advance tourism took place in 1975, when Cheyenne hosted the National Little Britches Finals Rodeo.

Accreditation with the U.S. Chamber of Commerce first occurred in 1976 and has been continued at five-year intervals.

In 1986 the chamber was active in the promotion and passage of the 2-percent Lodging Tax to promote tourism. The Cheyenne Area Visitors Council (CAVC) was formed in 1987 with that same goal in mind. The year 1988 was an auspicious one for tourism due to increased promotion by the Visitors Council. The Cheyenne Street Railway Trolley was a welcome addition.

The chamber worked through task forces to establish a strong economic development effort

during 1985 and 1986. In order to ensure special emphasis, a separate organization, Cheyenne LEADS, was formed. The chamber continues its efforts to enhance the community and works closely with LEADS and CAVC to help them accomplish their specific goals.

Leadership Cheyenne, a program designed to give future leaders of the community a background on its daily operations, became a reality in 1985.

In 1988 the "Positively Cheyenne" campaign was kicked off to encourage a more positive attitude and atmosphere.

The chamber's history is the history of the City of Cheyenne. Cheyenne's goals, ambitions, and hopes are also that of the Greater Cheyenne Chamber of Commerce. Through the past 60-some years these aims have not varied from those expressed in the preamble to the bylaws adopted by the Industrial Club of Cheyenne in January 1907:

The objects of said corporation shall be and are to further and promote the business, commercial, and industrial interest of the City of Cheyenne; . . . to enhance the attractiveness of said City and its advantages as a place of residence to locate any business enterprises . . . and in general, to do any and all things that tend to advance the business, social, and intellectual life of said City; and to enable it the more successfully to accomplish its main purpose, said corporation shall have power.

CHEYENNE FRONTIER DAYS

Every July, during the last full week in the month, Cheyenne reverts back to its storied past in what has become one of the nation's largest and most famous western celebrations—Frontier Days.

Right: Willie Nelson was one of the most popular performers for the Frontier Days night shows.

Below: Bareback riding at the rodeo. The rider must remain on the back of the bucking horse for eight seconds minimum to have a chance at purse money.

For more than 90 years—beginning in 1897—this celebration has been going on and has steadily grown with the community. A one-day celebration in that first year, it started what has now become a 10-day extravaganza without rival.

The focus for Frontier Days is, and always will be, the rodeo. It features the very best Professional Rodeo Cowboys and the very best of all the stock contractors in a three-hour performance each afternoon that never stops moving.

But the entire show has grown into a family participation celebration that features such other activities as free pancake breakfasts three mornings during the week, parades on four of the mornings, and daily evening shows.

Right: Bull riding at the rodeo. A clown distracts the bull so that when the rider goes off, he can escape before the bull takes his revenge.

The night shows are highlighted by current top-name western music entertainers with an occasional rock group thrown in for the younger audience. The night activities get started with what has come to be known as "Thunder From the North"—chuckwagon racing. The Southern Plains Indian dancers also perform before the warm July days turn into cool summer evenings and the stage show entertainment begins.

All the while the carnival midway offers the best in carnival rides and concessions; more than 200 exhibitors show and sell their wares.

More than the event itself is the process by which it is put together each year. Frontier Days maintains a paid staff of only a few people, while in excess of 2,000 volunteers work countless hours throughout the year to plan, prepare, and run the show.

Cheyenne Frontier Days is the epitome of community pride and volunteerism; but even more than that, it is a tradition based on the history of the city and the West. It is truly "The Daddy of 'Em All."

MEMORIAL HOSPITAL OF LARAMIE COUNTY

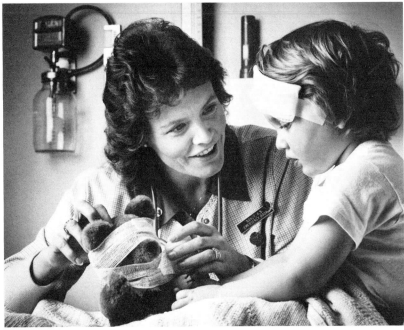

During its early history Memorial Hospital changed locations several times before becoming established at its current site in 1882. It began as a tent hospital, constructed by the Union Pacific Railroad in 1867 to treat workers injured while building the transcontinental railroad. One year later the founding fathers of Cheyenne purchased the tent for $125, establishing what is known today as Memorial Hospital of Laramie County.

From these beginnings the new City Hospital was soon set up in a 24-foot by 30-foot, two-story building, erected at a cost of $2,500 and designed to accommodate 40 patients. By 1870 the facility had again relocated, this

Top left: The first permanent county hospital building was constructed at 23rd Street and Evans Avenue in 1882 on land donated by the Union Pacific Railroad.

Top right: An artist's rendition of Memorial Hospital's Health Build 2000 project, scheduled for completion in the spring of 1989.

Bottom: Putting patients at ease is one of the many and varied responsibilities of the nurses at Memorial Hospital. Here, an emergency room nurse explains medical procedures to a youngster.

time to a building on the corner of 18th and O'Neil known as the Dodge House.

In 1882 the hospital found a permanent home in a new building constructed on a plot of prairie land donated by the Union Pacific Railroad—land that would eventually become the corner of 23rd Street and Evans Avenue.

By the year 1900 the institution had been renamed St. John's Hospital, and additions were made to the building in 1906 and 1911. First a maternity ward, furnished by the Women's Aid Society of Cheyenne, was added, then a wing was built by the Union Pacific Railroad to be used in caring for its employees.

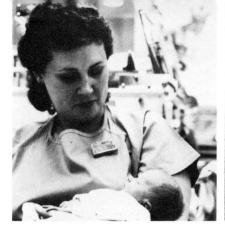

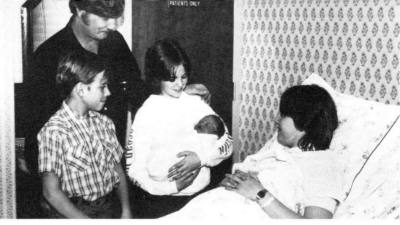

In 1919 St. John's was incorporated by Laramie County. Two years later the old hospital was torn down and a new, four-story brick building erected in its place.

In memory of the wife of General John "Black Jack" Pershing, the new structure was renamed Frances Warren Pershing Memorial Hospital of Laramie County. Mrs. Pershing, who was the daughter of Wyoming Senator F.E. Warren, had been killed in a fire in San Francisco's Presidio in 1915.

The first major remodeling of the 1923 building came in 1946, when a bond issue was passed providing for a south-facing extension to the hospital. Housed in this new addition were surgical areas, a new nursery, and labs for pathology and radiology.

A clinical laboratory was added to the hospital in 1957,

Top left: Infants receive plenty of tender loving care and affection in the Intensive Care Nursery.

Top right: In Memorial Hospital's birthing rooms the entire family can share in the first days of their newborn's life.

Below: Physical therapy personnel help a recent amputee learn to walk with his new prosthesis.

made possible by a donation from the Richardson family. One year later another bond issue provided funding for three more floors to be built above the Richardson Laboratory, a project that was completed in 1960 and forms the east wing of the hospital complex.

In 1968 Memorial Hospital completed the six-story West Tower, housing physical therapy, radiology, dietary facilities, the cafeteria, nursery and obstetrics, and patient rooms. In 1985 a radiation therapy addition housing a linear accelerator for the treatment of cancer was added to the West Tower.

In 1986 the fourth floor of the East Wing was remodeled to accommodate an 18-bed psychiatric unit for adults. That same year the hospital began construction on Health Build 2000, a $20-million expansion and modernization designed to provide Cheyenne and Laramie County residents with access to up-to-date medical facilities to the year 2000 and into the twenty-first century. Financing for the project was provided through the hospital's capital reserve fund and the sale of revenue bonds.

The project, completed in the spring of 1989, includes new areas for surgery, medical and surgical intensive care, major and minor emergency care, cardiopulmonary and neurology services, physical therapy, diagnostic radiology, obstetrics, laboratory facilities, and various hospital support services. Also

included is renovation to create new pharmaceutical, medical records, maintenance, and materials management departments.

The facilities are designed to accommodate the way in which hospital care will be delivered in the future, emphasizing outpatient services such as same-day surgery and emergency care. Rooms are designed to accommodate new and sophisticated equipment.

In 1987 the hospital obtained an argon endo-laser, the first of its kind in the state. The laser is used in conjunction with surgery to treat eye disorders brought on by diabetes, for certain types of retinal detachment, and treatment of rare types of glaucoma.

January 1988 saw the addition of a hyperthermia unit for the treatment of cancerous tumors; later that month an oncology unit opened at Memorial Hospital to provide specialized nursing care exclusively for cancer patients. This unique treatment program includes patient education; coordination between nursing staff, family, and patient; and facilities to enable family members to participate in total care of the patient. Sleeping accommodations and kitchen facilities, as well as support services, are available to family members.

With more than 120 years of providing quality, community-based health care to the residents of Cheyenne and Laramie County, Memorial Hospital is preparing to continue its tradition into the twenty-first century.

AMERICAN WYOTT CORPORATION

American Wyott Corporation is located at 1938 Wyott Drive, Cheyenne.

The American Wyott Corporation, a division of Associated American Industries of Dallas, Texas, is a leading employer in Cheyenne as well as the state of Wyoming. The American Wyott Corporation is both a manufacturer and developer of commercial food-service equipment, industrial equipment, and custom equipment. What sets the corporation apart from all others in the United States is a strong foundation based on research and development as well as a strong manufacturing capability in all disciplines.

American Wyott Corporation is proud to be a key supplier to many of the top 500 corporations in the United States, many front-range corporations and businesses as well as all major restaurant chains and institutions.

In the early 1930s a plumber sat in a Casper, Wyoming, restaurant and watched a waitress pour cream into tiny containers. The process was inefficient as much of the cream was wasted. The plumber's mind flashed back to the time he had repaired an Iowa farmer's well pump. At that time he had conceived the principle of the floating cylinder. That day in the restaurant he had found a practical use for his invention.

That was the origin of the first Wyott product—a cream dispenser. It was also the foundation of the Wyott Manufacturing Company: "WYO" for Wyoming and "TT" for the founders, Thomas L. Titus, the plumber/inventor, and Lewis C. Thomas, company president.

In February 1970 the Horst brothers—Paul, Ralph, and Alex—purchased the Wyott Manufacturing Company. They occupied the original buildings, one on 16th Street, the other on 18th Street. That same year the firm's name was changed to Wyott Corporation.

In 1971 a steamlined, efficient manufacturing operation emerged after a period of rapid expansion. New facilities were built consisting of 200,000 square feet for manufacturing and 7,000 for administrative offices. Expansion included various new product lines, such as overhead venting units, work tables, bins, deep-fat fryers, and custom-made products.

In August 1977 AMF, Inc., based in White Plains, New York, acquired the Wyott Corporation. While AMF was better known for

its leisure/recreational business, the firm also owned several industrial manufacturing plants. One of these plants was located in Essex, Connecticut, and served the food-service industry. AMF moved the facility and some of the employees to Cheyenne shortly after the acquisition.

AMF Wyott was sold in June 1986 to Associated American Industries of Dallas, Texas. Associated American Industries also owns American Permanent Ware of Dallas, another manufacturer of food-service equipment. At that time the company's name became American Wyott Corporation.

Currently American Wyott has more than 800 products in its standard catalog and is instrumental in customer product design and manufacture for major restaurants and fast-food chains. The company has expanded worldwide in the food-service industry. The present product line includes condiment pumps and containers, combination dispenser stands, cream and butter dispensers, hot dog cookers, refrigerated/freezer drawers, bun and food warmers, fryers and griddles, self-leveling dishware dispensers (mobile and in-counter), mobile snack carts, hot dog wagons, compactors, industrial dispensers, a line of food-holding and display cabinets, and a comprehensive client list of custom-designed and manufactured products.

William Schneider, president of American Wyott Corporation, and everyone at the company are pleased to be an important element in the future growth of Cheyenne and Wyoming.

LARAMIE COUNTY COMMUNITY COLLEGE

Laramie County Community College is looking toward the future with a growing enrollment, facilities that will allow expansion, and a sense that it is reaching out in new directions.

On May 21, 1968, Laramie County voters approved creation of the college to help fill a need for technical training and postsecondary education in the county. It continues to fill these needs even as the needs have changed over the years.

At that May election seven people from a field of 46 were elected to the first board of trustees. A nonprofit foundation was established by the board immediately to enable the new institution to receive gifts of money and real property and scholarship funds, and to offer other support to the college. Classes were scheduled to start in three new buildings in September 1969 at the college's permanent site southeast of Cheyenne.

However, construction was delayed, so LCCC's registration and classes in the fall of 1969 took place in local churches. Enrollment was 1,217, including full-time and part-time credit class and community service class students. Courses were offered in 19 academic and vocational areas.

Early in November 1969 the college moved into its new buildings at its present location of 1400 East College Drive. Those three structures are the present Administration, Classroom A, and Welding buildings.

Over the years rapid changes have taken place, most visible in growth of physical facilities, but also in development, improve-

ment, and initiation of educational programs. At present LCCC offers 55 programs leading to associate of arts, associate of science, or associate of applied science degrees or certificates of completion. In addition, basic skills, English as a second language, citizenship preparation, and G.E.D. preparation classes are offered at the Adult Learning Centers in Cheyenne and Laramie.

Facilities consist of 18 buildings constructed with financing provided by bond issues approved in 1972 and 1979, along with state and federal mineral funds supplemented by revenue bonds issued through the foundation. Total enrollment in all programs conducted by the college is more than 5,000 students.

In May 1986 LCCC and the University of Wyoming signed a cooperative agreement under which LCCC would provide pre-college math and English courses in Laramie through LCCC's Laramie Outreach Center, and UW would offer junior- and senior-level courses on the LCCC campus. It also made it possible for students to earn a bachelor's degree in office administration in Cheyenne.

Now the youngest of Wyoming's seven community colleges is also its second largest in enrollment. Laramie County Community College's goals include increased cooperation with other colleges and universities in the region, innovative programs to meet the employment needs of area business and industry, and proposed additions in the form of a modern science building and on-campus student housing.

Above: The Wyoming state flag shares the flagpole with the Stars and Stripes in front of the Laramie County Community College Administration Building.

Below: A young dancer entertains hungry picnickers lined up at an All-College Barbecue. The event is held each spring to round out the school year and again in the fall to usher in the new academic year.

FRONTIER OIL AND REFINING COMPANY

An aerial view of The Frontier Refining Company as it appeared in 1961.

In 1937 a new name had entered the refining industry—Bay Petroleum Company. Bay was a refining firm organized by young Nebraska oilman M.H. "Bud" Robineau and his brother-in-law, C.U. Bay, a former United States Ambassador to Sweden, who consented to lending his name to the Denver-based company, which owned a small refinery in Cheyenne.

On June 12, 1940, The Frontier Refining Company was formed as successor to Bay Petroleum by M.H. Robineau, Roland V. Rodman, and Brad Ferrall. At the time The Frontier Refining Company was organized, the Cheyenne Refinery was just a small plant with a thruput capacity of only 1,800 barrels per day. But as World War II closed in on America, progress was about to hit the little Cheyenne Refinery with a bang.

An edition of the December 1943 *Cheyenne Eagle* shows a blurry photo of a group of men kneeling in front of The Frontier Refining Company's Cheyenne alkylation pump house and alkylation fractionation area. The headline on the accompanying article reads: "These men are homefront soldiers who are helping shorten the war." The piece went on to report that a total of 825 men were working to beat a construction deadline on Frontier Refining's multimillion-dollar, 100-octane gasoline unit. The enlarged and modernized plant did an outstanding wartime job of producing aviation gasoline, and, in the process, it grew larger.

When the war was over Frontier made a favorable purchase of the government-built aviation fuel facilities and converted them to produce commercial-grade gasolines and fuel oils. The refinery was continuously maintained and revamped, and other units added so that by 1966 the refining complex included crude and vacuum distillation, fluid catalytic cracking, polymerization, platforming, unifining, and merox treating processes. That year a new propane deasphalting unit was constructed, and the plant was rated at 20,000 barrels per day (bpd).

Husky Oil Company assumed ownership of The Frontier Refining Company in February 1968 and initiated a major modernization project three years later. By the end of 1972 the crude capacity had been increased, and a new, 2,700-barrel-per-day hydrofluoric acid alkylation unit, a 1,500-barrel-per-day butamer unit, a 7,500-barrel-per-day hydrotreater, and a 6,500-barrel-per-day ' reformer had been added. By the end of 1974 the crude capacity had been increased to 24,000 barrels per day, and the modernization program had included design elements for meeting new pollution-control regulations.

In 1977 a fully automated, in-line gasoline blending unit with a capacity of 3,000 barrels per hour was installed, and a new computerized-transport, driver-operated, bottom-loading, vapor-recovery light-oil products loading dock was added. A loading facility was completed and in full use by January 1978, and a new, claus sulfur recovery unit was finished in October 1979. Construction of a new crude unit was completed in October 1979 and a coker erected a year later.

The new crude unit increased capacity by 25 percent, from 24,000 barrels per day to 30,000 barrels per day, while replacing three old crude units and reducing emissions and plant energy requirements. Delayed coking facilities allowed the refinery considerable flexibility in determining which crudes may be run, while improving the mixture of products produced.

In 1984 Husky Oil, Ltd., of Calgary decided to sell its downstream U.S. operations. On February 28, 1986, the Cheyenne refinery was purchased by a group of independent investors, who renamed it Frontier Oil and Refining Company. They also revived the former red-and-white Frontier logo by adding to it a silhouette of a cowboy on a bucking horse.

The new owners committed $8 million to an environmental program. Air-pollution-control changes are now complete, and wastewater problems are being addressed.

Today the Cheyenne refinery does not bear much similarity to the old, original company, although it is still located where it began, on the southeast side of town. Continual expansion and modernization has turned the refinery into a computerized, automated refinery, processing 35,000 barrels per day of crude oil into a variety of petroleum products for use in southern Wyoming, western Nebraska, and the Colorado Front Range.

Frontier Oil's Cheyenne refinery employs 190 people at the plant site. Its flexible processing capabilities enable it to produce three grades of gasoline (regular leaded, regular unleaded, and premium unleaded), three grades of diesel fuel, all grades of asphalt, propane, and petroleum coke.

The Cheyenne refinery normally produces 650,000 gallons of gasoline and about 400,000 gallons of diesel fuel per day. These two products account for more than 85 percent of the total

products shipped from the plant. Approximately one-half of the production is shipped via Continental Pipeline, which travels east to Nebraska, and WYCO Pipeline, which travels south to Colorado. The remaining product is distributed locally and throughout southern Wyoming by truck. The refinery's products are sold to major oil companies as well as smaller independents that have retail operations in the region.

The third-largest private employer in the Cheyenne area, Frontier Oil's refinery has long had a positive economic impact on the local community. The firm maintains a multifaceted role as an important local job source, concerned corporate citizen, and regional supplier of quality petroleum products.

A construction crew on December 11, 1943. The National Defense Plant Corporation built a modern structure adjacent to the existing facility to produce high-octane aviation fuel for military use.

TCI CABLEVISION OF WYOMING, INC.

Cheyenne's cable television system was originally built in 1968 by Bill Grove, who named his new operation Frontier Broadcasting.

On January 9, 1984, Frontier Broadcasting was acquired by Tele-Communications Inc., and became TCI Cablevision of Wyoming, Inc., in 1987. TCI had been founded by Bob Magness in 1956, the first cable system in Memphis, a small town in the Texas Panhandle.

Magness explains, "I picked up some characters one night down at the cotton gin . . . they had lost their ride and I visited with them . . . They had just built their first cable system.

"The next morning I went down and talked some more with those folks—they were nice people—and they got out the books and showed me who to get in touch with . . . and in 30 or 40 days, I was in business."

Magness built up that first cable system in Memphis to 600 or 700 subscribers in a year or so, and then moved on to Montana in 1958 to develop cable properties there. Six years later, in 1964, Bob and his wife, Betsy, merged their Montana and Texas interest with the Standard Corporation of Ogden, the Kearns Corporation of Salt Lake City, and the Copper Broadcasting Company of Butte. They named the new venture Community Television, Inc.

Those remote areas needed microwave, so a microwave business emerged alongside the cable business to supply signals to systems owned by Community Television. In August 1968 Magness and his associates merged the interest of the two groups to form Tele-Communications, Inc.

Corporate offices moved to Denver in fall 1965, and Bob bought a ranch in the Colorado mountains west of Denver. Most of his time is still spent working at the corporate headquarters in Denver or in business travel.

TCI is currently the nation's largest cable operating company, providing service to more than 3 million subscribers, with 600 cable systems throughout 45 states.

The Cheyenne cable system is undergoing a total upgrading—in excess of 300 miles of cable—in anticipation of future customer needs. As well as providing basic and premium programming to the Cheyenne community, TCI is heavily involved in community service.

The firm participates in the annual Muscular Dystrophy campaign by donating all income gained from installations over a four-month period to the local Muscular Dystrophy chapter. TCI also is active in the annual Toys for Tots campaign. In 1987 more than 1,000 toys were given through TCI—the largest donation from a local Cheyenne organization. For the annual Safe House Auction, TCI donates a painting and one year of free cable service. In addition to contributing annually to community nonprofit campaigns, TCI has given X*Press X*Change software to Cheyenne schools to enable reception of news features and informational sources.

TCI Cablevision of Wyoming, Inc., has more than 30 local employees in Cheyenne, and operates 14 cable systems in Wyoming. Francis E. Warren Air Force Base was added in 1986 to the local Cheyenne system.

TCI Cablevision of Wyoming, Inc., serving Cheyenne, owns and operates this satellite receiving equipment containing video-ciphers, modulators, a civil emergency alert system, FM equipment, and information storage. The cable TV company operates three such receiving stations placed in different areas around Cheyenne. This particular equipment became a major part of maintaining Cheyenne's picture quality in 1984. Photo by Richard L. Collier

CHEYENNE AERO TECH

Above: Students completely tear down and rebuild all the parts of an aircraft as part of their training process.

Above left: Students assembled from scratch, designed the paint scheme, and painted this MU2 donated to the school by Mitsubishi.

During the past five years Cheyenne Aero Tech has trained hundreds of aviation maintenance technicians for careers in the aviation industry.

Cheyenne Aero Tech opened its doors in August 1983 with an initial enrollment of 200. Today the school has more than 350 students. The institution attracts students from all over the United States and worldwide—some from as far away as Canada, Hong Kong, and Germany.

The students' average age is 27. Many work part time or are involved in community activities. To assist students with tuition costs, Cheyenne Aero Tech has an active Financial Aid Department and Job Placement Program. Because many students relocate to Cheyenne to enroll in the Aero Tech program, the school has a great financial impact on the community.

Located on airport property, at 3801 Morrie Avenue, the facility encompasses 48,000 square feet of classroom, shop, and student service areas. Owned by a California-based company, United Education and Software,

which operates 33 schools nationwide, Cheyenne Aero Tech produces highly qualified students by providing expert instructors and staff. For hands-on instruction, the school maintains a variety of state-of-the-art equipment and aircraft, including a Cessna 150 and 172, Apache PA23, Piper PA-28-180, Bell 47G helicopter, and a Mitsubishi MU2 turboprop aircraft.

The Cheyenne Aero Tech faculty consists of 16 experienced instructors and a total staff of 45. While most aviation programs are 18 to 24 months long, Aero Tech's intensive program allows students to complete the program in 12 months. Upon completion of the program, students take a series of written and oral exams before being certified as an aviation maintenance technician.

The rigorous Aero Tech program demands that students be highly motivated—the school day runs eight hours and class attendance is mandatory. Aero Tech students are also highly committed to the program: The school's dropout rate is less than 3 percent, far below the national average.

Through the years Cheyenne Aero Tech has established a solid reputation with the nation's airlines, airport operations, and aircraft manufacturers. One indication of this reputation is the fact that more than 90 percent of available Aero Tech graduates find employment in the aviation industry. About 70 percent of its graduates are hired by the major airlines; 18 percent go to regional and commuter airlines, fixed-base operators, and the helicopter industries; 5 percent are employed by aircraft manufacturers; 5 percent continue their education; and 2 percent enter the military.

According to experts, the employment outlook for aviation mechanics is excellent. In addition to industry growth, it is estimated that 50,000 veteran mechanics will retire in the next few years. With the need for skilled, well-trained aviation mechanics expected to soar, the outlook for Cheyenne Aero Tech and its graduates appears ready to take off.

WYOMING HEREFORD RANCH

CHRONOLOGY

WYOMING HEREFORD ASSOCIATION

—1883-1887— Owners: Alexander H. Swan, Thomas Swan, George F. Morgan & Associates, Manager: George F. Morgan.

—1887-1890— In receivership, In charge: Sheriff Sharpless, succeeded January 1888 by Colin Hunter, Foreman: William J. Rossman.

—1890-1916— Owners: Henry Altman, Dan McUlvan, Forman: Will Rossman.

HEREFORD CORPORATION OF WYOMING

—1916-1921— Owners: James D. and Raymond S. Husted, Superintendent: Will Rossman.

WYOMING HEREFORD RANCH

—1921-1938— Owner: Henry Parsons Crowell, Managers: Robert W. and Edward Lazear.

—1938-1957— Owner: Wyoming Hereford Ranch Foundation, a Crowell trust, Managers: Robert W. Lazear, Edward Lazear co-manager some years.

—1957-1958— Owners: Mr. and Mrs. Thomas E. Leavey and G.C. Parker, Manager: Robert W. Lazear until his death January 25, 1957, George Lazear.

—1958-1967— Owners: Mr. and Mrs. Thomas E. Leavey, Manager: George Lazear, succeeded by Lloyd Breisch.

—1967-1976— Owner: Neilson Enterprises Inc., Manager: Lloyd Breisch until his death February 1968, Ed Williams until June 1968, Ted Thomas June 1968-1974, Bill Wadlow, 1974-1976.

—1976-1978— Owner of the land: Nielson Enterprises, leased by Sloan and Anna Marie Hales, Manager: R.C. Bishop.

—1978-PRESENT— Owners: Sloan and Anna Marie Hales, Manager: David H. Forth, succeeded by Dick Davis.

Above left: A view of Wyoming Hereford Ranch, southeast of Cheyenne.

Bottom: The famous Lerch, a product of WHR, has offspring in herds throughout the country.

Above: Sloan and Anna Marie Hales and their children.

James Michener stayed there while he researched *Centennial.* Wyoming Hereford Ranch is the oldest major continuing, registered Hereford operation in North America.

During more than 100 years of operation—with a succession of owners and despite economic and natural disasters—WHR has endured and prospered, keeping alive the goals and dreams of the original founder, Alexander Swan.

Alexander Hamilton Swan incorporated his Wyoming Hereford Association in 1883. It was later to become Hereford Corporation of Wyoming, and finally Wyoming Hereford Ranch. The ranch has been breeding registered Herefords continuously since then, and continues to this day.

When Swan, owner of Two Bar Ranch at Chugwater, Wyoming, was ready to stock his new acreage southeast of Cheyenne, he sent ranch manager George F. Morgan to England for the foundation herd. Among western stockgrowers at that time, this was a controversial move.

Drought, inflation, disastrously low prices, and the calamitous blizzards of 1886-1887 combined to bankrupt the Wyoming Hereford Association.

Thus began a succession of owners until the ranch was purchased by Sloan and Anna Marie Hales in 1978. In 1983 the Hales family moved into the newly constructed Hereford Manor—the first owners to actually reside on the historic 100-year-old ranch property.

BURLINGTON NORTHERN RAILROAD

Burlington Northern Railroad and its predecessors have been important parts of Wyoming's transportation system ever since the Chicago, Burlington & Quincy Railroad completed its first main line through northeastern Wyoming in the 1890s.

The system developed further after the turn of the century, when acquisition of the Colorado & Southern/Fort Worth & Denver provided Wyoming with a line south to the Gulf Coast, and a second main line was completed through the Bighorn Basin to Casper.

As Wyoming developed its energy resources, Burlington Northern developed its transportation network. More than $1.5 billion went to strengthen coal-hauling corridors in the 1970s, and late in the decade BN completed its Gillette-Orin line to serve the mines of the Powder River Basin.

BN Railroad moves millions of tons of Wyoming coal to markets as far distant as the Great Lakes, Gulf Coast, and Southeast. Low-cost unit train transportation allows Powder River coal to compete with coals and other fuels higher in heat value and closer to end-use markets.

In 1986 BN's first installation of concrete ties on heavy tonnage routes occurred in Wyoming, opening a new era for the entire railroad industry.

BN provides its Wyoming customers with direct train service to the Pacific Northwest, Midwest, and the south-central part of the United States, moving much of the country's food, cars, building materials, chemicals, coal, and many other everyday things necessary for life and comfort.

BN is a leader in intermodal transportation, which uses both trucks and rail to provide quality, cost-efficient service, working closely with major ports throughout the country to assure quick shipment of international goods.

BN operates around the clock, with 700 trains per day in 25 states and two Canadian provinces. BN works to advance the technology of transportation, presently testing a system that uses communications satellites to improve control of train movements. Many BN locomotives use microcomputer-based control systems.

Of BN's 32,000 employees nationwide, more than 1,500 call Wyoming home, and they have the skills to keep Burlington Northern Railroad changing in response to Wyoming's changing transportation needs. They also are active in civic and charitable activities.

BN feels a strong commitment to the more than 4,000 communities it serves. Its philanthropic arm, Burlington Northern Foundation, donates close to $13 million annually to help educational institutions, cultural organizations, human-service programs, civic services, youth programs, hospitals, and United Way programs. Every year 1.5 percent of Burlington Northern Inc.'s pretax income goes to the foundation to support these causes.

Burlington Northern's loaded unit coal trains pause at the Guernsey, Wyoming, fueling station en route to their destinations at steam electric generating plants.

SWEDE'S ROOFING

"This is a strange business we've got here," is the way owner Harold "Swede" Mauch describes his roofing business. The ebb and flow of demand frequently coincides with the weather, hail and wind storms bringing boom times to the roofers.

Swede's business had a strange beginning. Swede and his partner were "boomers"—working wherever the demand for roofers took them. In late May 1955, on their way through Cheyenne to Montana, the two men stopped during the Memorial Day weekend. By the time the party was over, Swede found himself stranded in Cheyenne without a vehicle. His partner had gone on without him.

Swede went to work for a Cheyenne roofing firm and lived in motels. Finally he saved enough money to buy himself a pickup truck, and that was the beginning of Swede's Roofing. He worked out of his truck, subcontracting for other firms, and continued to live a wild life in motels.

In 1958 Swede met Betty Pitts in Riverton, Wyoming, where he had gone on a roofing job. They married and returned to Cheyenne, where Betty set up an office in their apartment and later in the house they bought in Sun Valley. Her first office consisted of an old treadle sewing machine used as a stand for her ancient Royal typewriter, and a legless coffee table top placed across two chairs for a desk. Swede, subcontracting for several roofing firms, worked throughout the state of Wyoming and eastern Nebraska.

In 1960 their son, Harold Jr.—known as J.R.—was born, and

A fleet of company trucks lines up in front of the warehouse of Swede's Roofing.

the following year saw another arrival, daughter Betty, who is nicknamed Penny.

Boeing Aircraft came to Cheyenne in the early 1960s, causing boom times for the local construction industry. Swede's crews roofed many of the residences in subdivisions that sprang up around Cheyenne. When Boeing left Cheyenne in the late 1960s, the economy slumped. Swede again sent his crews on jobs throughout the state—wherever roofers were needed, there went Swede. And Betty maintained the "living room office" at home.

Swede's Roofing went into the 1970s with its crews working away from home more than in Cheyenne. In those years buying materials was difficult without a credit history. It proved so hard to work with local lumberyards that materials were bought from a Colorado wholesale company and transported in trucks to Wyoming in order to complete projects.

By 1972 Cheyenne's economy was picking up, and the roofing business along with it. Swede and Betty invested in heavy trucks. The first two-ton company truck was purchased in 1970 and has ex-

panded to a fleet of four two-ton trucks, one with a boom; four pickups; and a forklift. In 1971 the couple moved to a house on Hansen Street and built a formal office onto their home.

By 1974 it became necessary to buy the operation's present site at 1130 Dunn Avenue and build a warehouse. Three years later the Mauches remodeled part of the warehouse for the present office. The "feast or famine" life-style has carried on into the present. When there is work to do, the family puts in 16-hour days and seven-day weeks.

When Swede's Roofing began in Cheyenne, there were four roofing companies in town; now there are 20 listings in Cheyenne and many firms have started up and died down. Swede and Betty point out with pride the roofs they are responsible for in Cheyenne, among them the Governor's Mansion, Little America, and the Nagle Mansion, which required the help of a cherry picker to complete. The company is proud of its reputation and its continuity.

TORTILLA MANUFACTURING AND SUPPLY/EL BRAVITO

John and Bonnie Turner, four of their children, and some of the children's spouses are all deeply involved in the family business. Another son runs the family ranch in western Colorado.

John Turner opened his first Mexican fast-food restaurant in the spring of 1968 in Cheyenne. Business was good, and it was not long before Taco John's, as the chain had come to be called, had several outlets in Cheyenne and other cities.

Although the food sold well, the tortillas available to the operation were not good enough. John's desire for the best drove him to "make my own tortillas"—and in 1969 Tortilla Manufacturing and Supply Co. was born. Bonnie and John made their tortillas using recipes from Bonnie's father, a retired baker. Their first manufacturing plant was in the garage behind their first taco restaurant.

John began his food-service career working for McDonald's. He later bought the Drift Inn on Logan Avenue, and expanded to ownership of seven drive-in

Here the tortillas are cooled and weighed before they are bagged for distribution.

restaurants in Cheyenne and Laramie, Wyoming; Lawrence, Kansas; and Dallas, Fort Worth, and Grand Prairie, Texas. Tacos looked like they were going to be popular, so John went into tacos. He built his first unit in Laramie while managing one of his drive-ins there, and moved the unit to Cheyenne to set up the first Taco John's on East Lincoln Way.

When he opened that restaurant, he had no signs up, and no one knew what it was. He put up an "Open" sign, and "people started coming in." Soon after that he began making his own tortillas.

In 1974 John designed a tortilla oven and cooling line that better suited his needs. He described his idea to Moline Manufacturing, a subsidiary of Pillsbury, and they custom-built his machine. Moline has since used his machine as a model for potential customers, and he continues to manufacture the machine.

Taco John's grew. Tortilla Manufacturing grew. Taco John's has grown to international proportions with 450 restaurants. Tortilla Manufacturing has sold more than one billion tortillas.

John Turner's interests in Taco John's were sold in 1985, and the family has since concentrated its efforts on the tortilla and chip manufacturing business.

Flour tortillas being cut for baking.

KFBC-KFBQ (Q98-FM)

KFBC, Cheyenne's first radio station, came into existence in 1940. Owned by the local newspaper at that time, the station concentrated predominantly on sports, news, and information.

In 1946 Larry Birleffi became associated with of the station, and in the late 1940s KFBC did the first live broadcast of a University of Wyoming football game. Since that time it has broadcast every University of Wyoming game. The Cowboy Sports Network originated with KFBC as its flagship station in those early days, and now-famous national sportscaster Curt Gowdy began his career announcing Wyoming football games over KFBC.

In 1977 Don Jones, an attorney from Torrington, and Larry Birleffi, bought the station. Then, in 1985, John Shideler bought out Jones and Birleffi; he now functions as the station's general manager. Shideler previously held the position of first vice-president in charge of operations for the Alf Landon Radio Station Group.

Birleffi is employed by the station and does sports and talk programs. Beginning in the 1960s the FM facility was expected to surpass the AM, and extensive remote capabilities have been added to allow broadcasts from a distance. A subsidiary, Broadcast Management Services, oversees operation of 12 other radio stations in the Rocky Mountain area.

The station continues today with its tradition of keeping Cheyenne citizens informed, and is busy expanding to more news, information, and talk shows. It has recently purchased a tool, known as color weather radar, to enable more specific weather analysis. KFBC-KFBQ is the first radio station to use this system to augment weather service forecasts with up-to-the-minute information. Beginning in January 1988 all station disk jockeys are being schooled to read this radar.

KFBC-KFBQ is a charter member of the ABC Radio Network, which, in the 1940s, split off from the NBC Network. The new network was originally known as the NBC Blue Network, but later became ABC.

KFBC-KFBQ enjoys the highest Arbitron rating in Cheyenne, with the number-one-rated personality, talk-show host Larry Peterson, who also covers the morning drive time. Arbitron is a national rating service for radio stations.

Tony Dee, program director for Q98-FM.

UNITED EXPRESS/ASPEN AIRWAYS

Right: A Convair 580, 50-passenger jet-powered aircraft flies regular Cheyenne-to-Denver and Cheyenne-to-Sheridan routes.

Air service began between Denver and Aspen in 1954, when a plane was purchased for the transportation of Aspen Institute for Humanistic Studies participants and members. Some years later this endeavor was purchased by a private interest, which became Aspen Airways. In late 1986 it became United Express, headquartered in Denver, Colorado.

On March 9, 1967, the company was given a Certificate of Convenience and Necessity by the Civil Aeronautics Board, which allowed it to operate large passenger aircraft exceeding the 12,500-pound limit, rather than the small air taxi equipment. In 1969 a Convair 240 was purchased, and 10 months later four Convair 340/440 were placed in service.

The firm has expanded to a fleet of 10 Convair 580s; they are jet powered, pressurized, radar equipped, and serviced by a

flight attendant on each flight. Four British Aerospace four-engine BAe 146-100 fanjet airliners were purchased, the first in December 1984, approximately two years before the company was identified as United Express. The BAe 146 aircraft are configured to hold 86 passengers and are serviced by two flight attendants.

The Convair 580s have two 4,000-horsepower jet engines and can fly at altitudes of 25,000 feet at 350 miles per hour. The 580 has a basic weight of 35,000 pounds and carries 50 passengers with a crew of three. The BAe 146 has four jet engines; it is considered the world's quietest aircraft.

Aspen Airways is a Colorado-owned and -operated airline. Flight crews must meet the same standards as United, American, TWA, and other Civil Aeronautics-based air carriers.

Aspen's United Express fleet consists of 14 aircraft painted in colors similar to United Airlines. The four BAe 146s and 10 Convair 580s are operated by Aspen

Above: Sporting its new paint scheme, this British aerospace 146 is the new, quiet 86-passenger jet acquired to enhance regional service.

Airways. All passengers who are members of United's Mileage Plus program receive a minimum of 500 miles on a United Express/Aspen Airways flight.

Aspen Airways operates scheduled flights between Denver and Aspen, Colorado Springs, Durango, Grand Junction, Gunnison, and Montrose, Colorado; Farmington, New Mexico; Rapid City, South Dakota; and Casper, Cheyenne, Cody, Gillette, Jackson Hole, and Sheridan, Wyoming.

Through fares on United and joint fares with other major carriers are offered on Aspen Airways scheduled flights. A VIP Room is provided for groups in Denver upon request. Aspen Airways flights are designated UA 3640 through 3999.

Aspen Airways also charters aircraft throughout the United States, Canada, the Caribbean, and Mexico.

A United Express route map.

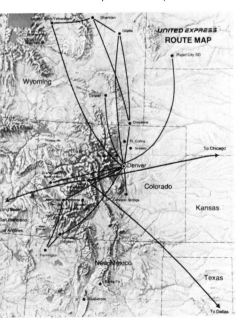

HOLIDAY INN CHEYENNE

The Holiday Inn Cheyenne opened in July 1981, providing the largest convention facilities in town, with a seating capacity of 1,200 people.

The 244 guest rooms include suites and handicapped facilities. There are two restaurants, a lounge, pool, whirlpool, saunas, and fitness center. John Q's restaurant features continental cuisine; 180 employees are required to run the complex.

The mover and shaker behind the establishment of Cheyenne's Holiday Inn is John Q. Hammons, a well-known philanthropist and developer from Springfield, Missouri. Hammons began his career in residential and commercial development in Springfield in 1949. Eager to expand his endeavors, he co-founded the firm of Winegardner & Hammons, Inc., in 1960 and ventured into Holiday Inn hotel development during its earliest stages. Nine years later he formed John Q. Hammons Industries to develop Holiday Inn hotels in the western part of the United States. Today his company owns and operates 36 Holiday Inn and Embassy Suite hotels in Arizona, Arkansas, California, Colorado, Illinois,

Iowa, Michigan, Missouri, Montana, New Mexico, Ohio, Oregon, North Carolina, South Carolina, South Dakota, Texas, Washington, and Wyoming.

Collectively, John Q. Hammons Industries and Winegardner & Hammons own and/or manage 80 hotels in 30 states where more than 15,000 rooms generate a gross volume of $250 million annually.

The Holiday Inn Cheyenne, at South Greeley Highway and Fox Farm Road.

In addition to the hotel development field, John Q. Hammons Industries has acquired many valuable real estate locations in various cities nationwide for future development in the residential, commercial, and industrial fields.

The firm presently has offices in Springfield, Missouri; Cincinnati, Ohio; and Sacramento, California.

In addition to his many business accomplishments, Hammons is well known and appreciated for his many philanthropic and charitable activities. Through the annual Salute to the Performing Arts, Hammons provides matching funds to those raised by the event to help underwrite local performing arts groups in Springfield.

He has contributed substantial support to the study and construction of the Hammons Heart Institute at St. John's Regional Health Center in Springfield; his donation of the Hammons Life Line emergency helicopter provided a new dimension in health care for the people of southwest Missouri.

Hammons' Founders Gift led to the establishment of Springfield's public television station and the Hammons School of Architecture on the campus of Drury College in Springfield. He also made possible construction of The Hammons House, a state-of-the-art student dormitory on the campus of Southwest Missouri State University. To honor their benefactor's many civic contributions, the City of Springfield changed the name of its Sherman Parkway to John Q. Hammons Parkway.

In 1987 Hammons received an honorary doctorate from Drury College. He was then elected to the Academy of Missouri Squires, which was founded by Governor James T. Blair, Jr., in 1960 to honor Missourians for their accomplishments of community, state, or national service. In late 1987 John Q. Hammons' name was included in the *Forbes* 400, in spite of his attempts to avoid being listed.

In March 1988 Springfield's District Court moved into the first privately built, owned, and operated courthouse in the country, thanks to John Q. Hammons. The unavailability of capital funds for new construction spawned the concept of leasing the space from a private developer rather than constructing a government-owned facility. Hammons got the bid, and built the courthouse for Springfield.

The lobby of the Holiday Inn Cheyenne.

PATRONS

The following individuals, companies, and organizations have made a valuable commitment to the quality of this publication. Windsor Publications and the Greater Cheyenne Chamber of Commerce gratefully acknowledge their participation in *Cheyenne: City of Blue Sky*.

American Wyott Corporation*

Burlington Northern Railroad*

Cheyenne Aero Tech*

Cheyenne Frontier Days*

Dineen Lincoln-Mercury-Subaru

Frontier Oil and Refining Company*

Holiday Inn Cheyenne*

KFBC-KFBQ (Q98-FM)*

Laramie County Community College*

Memorial Hospital of Laramie County*

Swede's Roofing*

TCI Cablevision of Wyoming, Inc.*

Tortilla Manufacturing and Supply/El Bravito*

United Express/Aspen Airways*

Wyoming Hereford Ranch*

*Partners in Progress of *Cheyenne: City of Blue Sky*. The histories of these companies and organizations appear in Chapter 7, beginning on page 105.

BOOKS AND PERIODICALS

Annals of Wyoming. Wyoming State Press, January 1946 and Fall 1982.

Apple, Charles, compiler. *Cheyenne Directory, 1895.* Cheyenne: The Leader Steam Print, 1895.

Bragg, Bill. *Wyoming's Wealth, A History of Wyoming.* Basin, Wyoming: Big Horn Book Co., 1976.

Bragg, Bill. *Wyoming: Rugged but Right.* Boulder, Colorado: Pruett Publishing Co., 1979.

Budd, Robert W. *Our First 100 Years.* Cheyenne, Wyoming: First National Bank and Trust Company of Wyoming, 1982

Cheyenne Historical Committee. *Cheyenne, the Magic City of The Plains 1867-1967.* Cheyenne Centennial Committee, 1967

Classified Business Directory. 1905-1906. R.L. Polk & Co. Publishers, 1906.

Garbarino, Merwyn S. *Native American History.* Little, Brown & Co., 1976.

Haley, John Paul, Jr. *A History of Laramie County School District #1.* Master's thesis, 1956.

Hanesworth, Robert D. *Daddy of 'Em All, The Story of Cheyenne Frontier Days.* Cheyenne, Wyoming: Flintlock Publishing Co, 1967.

Hanson, Con. *I Remember, Stories of Wyoming.* M/M Conrad Hanson, 1967.

Jensen, Oliver. *The American Heritage History of Railroads in America.* New York: American Heritage Publishing Co., 1975.

Johnson, A.R., compiler. *Residence and Business Directory of Cheyenne, 1884-1885.* Cheyenne, Wyoming: The Leader Printing Co., 1885.

Jones, Gladys Powelson. *Cheyenne, Cheyenne, Our Blue Collar Heritage.* Gladys Powelson Jones, 1983.

Larson, T.A. *History of Wyoming.* Second Edition, Revised, Lincoln and London: University of Nebraska Press, 1978.

Reps, John W. *Cities of The American West, A History of Frontier Urban Planning.* Princeton, N.J.: Princeton University Press.

Saltiel, E.H., and Barnett, George. *History and Business Directory of Cheyenne, 1868.* L.B. Joseph, Bookseller & Publisher, 1868.

Spiegel, Sydney. *History of Laramie County, Wyoming to 1890.* A thesis, University of Wyoming, 1961.

Trenholm, Virginia Cole and Carley, Maureen. *Wyoming Pageant.* Casper, Wyoming: Baily School Supply, 1946.

Wedel, Waldo R. *Prehistoric Man on The Great Plains.* Norman, Oklahoma: University of Oklahoma Press, 1961.

Wyoming State Business Directory, 1917. Denver, Colorado: The Gazeteer Publishing and Printing Co., 1917.

Wyoming State Historical Society. *Early Cheyenne Homes, 1880-1890.* Compiled by the Laramie County Chapter of the Wyoming State Historical Society (Cheyenne: 1962, 1964, 1975). Revised Edition published by the Wyoming State Press, Cheyenne, 1983.

Stock Growers National Bank was founded in 1881, and opened for business in 1882 in the Carey Block. It was common practice to name blocks after the original builder of the buildings, which often consisted of one continous building taking up the whole block, and divided into a number of businesses. Courtesy, Wyoming State Archives, Museums and Historical Department

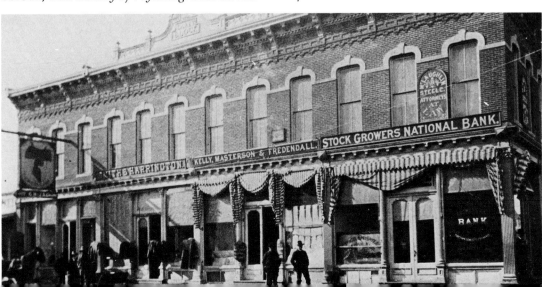

Index